Praise for *My Sc*

In this inspiring, elegantly written, and deeply experiential journey through the Psalms of the Advent season, Father Martin Shannon takes us on a pilgrimage within. In the silence, peace, and watchfulness of Advent, this book is a steady and enriching guide to the great feast of the Savior's birth.

—ABBOT PRIMATE GREGORY POLAN, OSB, Sant Anselmo, Rome,
Primate of the Benedictine Confederation

Reading the psalms daily year by year, season by season is formative. Before you know it your thinking and perceiving about God, about the world and everyone in it, about who you yourself are, will steadily be transformed.

—MARY COLLINS, OSB, Past Prioress of Mount St. Scholastica,
Professor Emerita of the School of Theology and Religious Studies at the
Catholic University of America, Washington, DC

Rightly convinced that the Psalms are prayers flowing from the soul of Christ—the author of this lovely book provides clear, correct, and succinct meditations on various psalms appropriately prayed during Advent and the Christmas season. The work is recommended without reserve.

—PATRICK HENRY REARDON, author of *Christ in the Psalms* and
senior editor, *Touchstone Magazine*

The author demonstrates his own knowledge of the original language of each psalm, its setting in history, and its common traditional interpretations, and then adds his own sensitive and enriching suggestions for our own understanding and prayerful use of each psalm.

—FR. JOHN-JULIAN, OJN, author of *The Complete Julian of Norwich*

My Soul Waits is a balm to the spirit, an honest companion for the soul's seasons of triumph and trembling, turmoil and tenderness.

—RACHEL G. HACKENBERG, author of *Writing to God* and *Sacred Pause*

Our soul waits for the Lord.
Psalm 33:20

 SOUL
WAITS

Praying with the Psalms through
Advent, Christmas & Epiphany

MARTIN SHANNON, CJ

PARACLETE PRESS
BREWSTER, MASSACHUSETTS

2017 First printing

My Soul Waits: Praying with the Psalms Through Advent, Christmas & Epiphany
Copyright © 2017 by Rev. Robert L. Shannon
ISBN 978-1-61261-970-5

Library of Congress Cataloging-in-Publication Data
Names: Shannon, Martin, author.
Title: My soul waits : praying with the Psalms through Advent, Christmas & Epiphany / Martin Shannon, CJ.
Description: Brewster, Massachusetts : Paraclete Press Inc., 2017. | Includes bibliographical references.
Identifiers: LCCN 2017030835 | ISBN 9781612619705 (trade paper)
Subjects: LCSH: Bible. Psalms--Devotional use. | Advent--Prayers and devotions. | Christmas--Prayers and devotions. | Epiphany--Prayers and devotions.
Classification: LCC BS1430.54 .S534 2017 | DDC 242/.33--dc23
LC record available at https://lccn.loc.gov/2017030835

10 9 8 7 6 5 4 3 2 1

Published by Paraclete Press
Brewster, Massachusetts
www.paracletepress.com

Printed in the United States of America

CONTENTS

Introduction

I N HIS RULE FOR MONASTIC LIFE, ST. BENEDICT WROTE
that the life of a monk should be like a continuous Lent
(chapter 49). He acknowledged that not everyone has the
strength to do this (how's that for understatement?), so, at least
during the liturgical season, he wanted his monks to take on some
additional and intentional acts of self-denial, all the while never
forgetting that the essential aim of Lent is to look forward to
Easter with joy and longing. Life has plenty of asceticism built
in already (most of it unexpected), and it is nothing if not a hope
and desire for resurrection in the end. So, even though he didn't,
perhaps Benedict could have said something similar about Advent.

I live in an ecumenical monastic community of both celibate
and married men and women, a modern expression of an ancient
way of life in which St. Benedict's voice keeps whispering insights
into our ears. The idea of seriously embracing the particular character of each liturgical season, though not exclusive to Benedict,
of course, is one of those insights. With the arrival of Advent, we
change the color of our vestments (we all wear albs and scapulars
to liturgy); our chants take on a new character; we begin to add
certain elements to our surroundings (the number of candles in the
church multiplies, for example); and, individually, we may take on
additional forms of personal prayer and fasting. And all the while,
we refuse to add Christmas carols to our repertoire of hymns until
we actually get to Christmas. We are fairly uncompromising about

that. Advent has its particular emphasis on preparation, getting
ready, longing for, making room, and we don't want to get ahead
of ourselves. The meaning is in the waiting. Arriving has its own
significance, and the two should not be confused.

So, yes, the life of a monk, or of any Christian for that matter, should be, and in fact is, a continual Advent. Until the day of
Christ's coming—either to re-enter this world with more splendor
than we can imagine, or to take us to his world (more splendorous
still)—we are limited to and gifted with lives of waiting.

One thing we do at the Community of Jesus while we wait,
through both the season of Advent and throughout our lives of
continuous Advent, is sing the psalms. The psalms are the prayers
and praises of people who started waiting long before we did, a
vocabulary given by heaven to help both them and us to learn
its language and to get ready to sing in its halls. As the world
spins, there is not a moment that passes in which the words of
the psalms, in any number of languages, are not being sung. The
whole world is waiting.

Except for a few places (such as the first day of Advent and
Christmas Day), the forty-one psalms in this collection are not
presented in any particular order. This is because neither your life
nor my life goes in any particular order either. The ascending and
descending notes of life are sounded mostly without warning, and
part of my learning to *get ready* and to *make room* is to go with these
ups and downs as they come, and to find in each one a new chord
for the "new song." The psalms are tried-and-true instruments upon
which the songs of my life can be played out while, in Advent and
in every other time, my soul waits.

REFLECTIONS

1

First Sunday of Advent
PSALM 33

Our soul waits for the Lord.

v. 20

THE FIRST WORD OF PSALM 33 IS ONE OF SIX WORDS for "praise" used by the author of this song. It first appears in Scripture in the book of Leviticus to describe the response of the Jewish assembly when the fire of God came down from heaven and consumed the offerings made by Moses and Aaron in the tent of meeting. When all the people saw the glory of the Lord unexpectedly appearing in this way, "they *shouted for joy* and fell facedown" (Lev. 9:24, NIV). This was a spontaneous cry of rejoicing, elicited by an extraordinarily dramatic sign of God's presence come among them.

Psalm 33 is a call to praise and worship. Unlike many psalms that were written in connection with specific circumstances, this psalm has a more general character. God's unwavering qualities of creative power, just rule, and loyal love are reason enough to shout for joy, as the psalmist says. Still, there are hints in verses 16 through 19 that all is not sweetness and light. There is a suggestion that war may be at hand, and with it the possibility of famine and death. It seems unlikely that the psalmist would write about hoping in God's deliverance unless there was some need of it: "Our soul waits for the Lord . . . our heart is glad in him, because we trust in his holy name" (Ps. 33:20–21). These are the words of people who sing to God, even while they look for help—who rejoice, even while they wait. Psalm 33 makes partners of patience and praise.

So, while they wait, the people sing, for, in all of creation and through all of history, they discern the life-giving hand of God at work—"the earth is *full* of the goodness of the Lord" (5, KJV). So full, it seems, that the earth cannot contain it all and joy bursts forth into a "new song" of praise to God. This is the first time in the Bible that the phrase "new song" appears. Together with only a few other occasions (notably Psalms 96, 98, and 149), it heralds the wondrous sound to be heard in heaven when the saints are gathered around the Lamb, when all rejoicing will be full and all waiting will be over: "I heard a voice from heaven like the sound of many waters and like the sound of loud thunder; the voice I heard was like the sound of harpers playing on their harps, and they sing a new song before the throne" (Rev. 14:2–3).

"And the Word became flesh and dwelt among us, full of grace and truth; we have beheld his glory, glory as of the only Son from the Father" (John 1:14). With these words, the Gospel of John describes the supremely extraordinary appearance of God's glory coming to fill all the earth—the incarnation of his only Son, Jesus Christ. The fire of God's love was ignited in the womb of a Virgin, and there kindled a flame intended to enlighten the hearts of all people. A cry of rejoicing is certainly a fitting response, even as we wait for that fire to come again. If I need a new visitation from the Almighty, if I look for a fresh appearance of his love—as I most certainly do every Advent—then Psalm 33 reminds me that my heart can (and *must*) rejoice, even as my soul waits.

FROM THE FATHERS

Strip off your oldness; you know a new song. A new person, a New Covenant, a new song. People stuck in the old life have no business with this new song; only those who are new persons can learn it, renewed by grace and throwing off the old, sharers in the kingdom of heaven. All our love yearns toward that kingdom, and in its longing our life sings a new song. Let us sing this song not only with our tongues, but with our lives.

Augustine

Re-tune my heart again, Lord
to the angels' key, and not my own.
Correct its tones, adjust its pitches, change its temperament,
—all by heaven's eternal "A."
While I wait,
re-tune my heart again, Lord.
Today's song should be new.

2

Monday of Advent I
PSALM 67

*May God be gracious to us and bless us
and make his face to shine upon us.*

v. 1

ARON AND THE LEVITICAL PRIESTHOOD WERE instructed to bless the people of Israel with these words: "The LORD bless you and keep you: The LORD make his face to shine upon you, and be gracious to you: The LORD lift up his countenance upon you, and give you peace" (Num. 6:24–26). Psalm 67 is a prayer of blessing that comes out of the same tradition. It sees the blessing of God as the very source of life and health, without which there is no hope for prosperity or peace.

A rich tone of thanksgiving is prevalent throughout the psalm, and this probably explains why it was used at the great autumn Feast of Sukkot, or Tabernacles. The feast is significant for two reasons. First, according to Exodus 34:22, it celebrates the "ingathering" of the harvest, the annual sign of God's blessing in the fruitfulness of the fields. "The earth has yielded its increase," declares the psalmist (Ps. 67:6), and in that plenty is seen the face of God. Second, the feast is a reminder of the Israelites' sojourn in the wilderness (Lev. 23:39–43), during which God "made the people of Israel dwell in booths," or *sukkot*, temporary huts built of branches and leafy boughs, as they made their way from one camp to another on their trek from Egypt to the Promised Land.

Together with a spirit of celebration, therefore, the brief verses of Psalm 67 confess a sense of utter dependence of the people of Israel—of all the nations, indeed of all the earth—on the favorable presence of God. As the psalmist says elsewhere about all created life, "When you give it to them they gather it up; when you open your hand, they are satisfied with good things. When you hide your face, they are terrified; when you take away their breath, they die and return to the dust" (Ps. 104:28–29, NIV).

In his rule for the monastic community, Saint Benedict prescribed Psalm 67 to be sung every morning at daybreak, the rising sun being an apt image for the radiant and life-giving face of God. Morning after morning, the day is prayerfully greeted by monks with this simple acknowledgment and petition: "Like the rising sun, O Lord, may your face shine upon us this new day, and bring us life. Bless us with the warmth of your presence and we, in turn, will reflect that blessing to others and we will praise your name forever." A prayer for God's blessing is never contingent upon dire circumstances, illness, or misfortune. It is appropriate to every day of our lives, for every day of life given to us is an act of God's mercy and favor.

FROM THE FATHERS

"The earth has yielded its fruit"—it has yielded a grain of wheat. Because the grain of wheat has fallen into the ground and died, it produces many fruits. The fruit is multiplied in the head of the grain. Because one has fallen, it rose again with many; one grain of wheat has fallen into the ground and a fruitful harvest came of it.

Jerome

Today I look to you for your blessing, Father.
My life is in your hands—
    may those hands hold me close, and keep me.
I also pray for your blessing upon all those who are dear to me—
    may your salvation be known to them today.
And for your blessing, Father, I offer my thanksgiving—
    may neither ever cease.

3

Tuesday of Advent I
PSALM 85

For he will speak peace to his people,
to his saints,
to those who turn to him in their hearts.

v. 8

SOMETHING IS AMISS IN THE LAND. IS IT A DROUGHT? Is it the threat of defeat at the hand of the enemy? Is it some sudden national disaster? All we know for sure is that something has gone desperately wrong, behind which the psalmist sees the hand of God's divine judgment. His appeal is simple yet fervent: "Restore us again, O God of our salvation, and put away thy indignation toward us!"

Upon what does the psalmist base his petition? He spends the opening verses of the song looking back upon multiple evidences of God's faithfulness and love for his people: God has already been gracious in delivering the land from captivity; he has shown his mercy in forgiving the people; the land has already known a peace that comes from the providential care of the Lord. As he rehearses this historical account of the nation's prosperity, it is as if the psalmist is *reminding* the Lord of how good he has already been to his people. A similar thing happens at the beginning of Psalm 44: "We have heard with our ears, O God, our fathers have told us, what deeds thou didst perform in their days, in the days of old" (44:1).

The thought of "reminding God" of anything seems, at first glance, at least presumptuous if not downright ridiculous. Who needs to—who dares to—remind the Creator of all time and space of what he has already done in days past? Yet, does not this kind of address to God indicate a depth of intimacy between the psalmist and his God, a depth of honesty and trust? Beyond its use as a poetic device, reminding God of the good things of the past is a way of opening ourselves to God's future: "Before I ask anything further of you, Lord, let me first remind you that you and I have been here before. Look what you have done for me already. Will you please do it again?"

In the end, of course, by "reminding" God of his goodness, the psalmist is, in fact "counting his blessings" in the presence of the one from whom all blessings flow. It is we, in fact, who need the reminding, so that in our need we can make our prayer with hope. Recalling the undeniable acts of God's love in our lives is part of what allows us also to offer him our genuine complaints. We can take our cue from the psalmist who, having reached out for help—"revive us again . . . grant us thy salvation" (6–7)—then sits back to wait and listen for the answer: "let me hear what God the LORD will speak" (8).

The psalmist writes as someone who knows that eventually the answer will be given and the word of peace will come, as simply and gently as a kiss on the cheek (10). And when it does, it will be added to the number of answers that the psalmist has already heard. A whole storehouse of God's answers is being gathered, always ready to be drawn upon as reminders whenever the next need arises and the next cry for help must be made.

FROM THE FATHERS

Until the Lord restores us to life, we are dead. "Show us, O Lord, your kindness, and grant us your salvation." The Savior's descent is the work of God's mercy. He would not have come as a physician if most people were not sick. Because so many were sick, he came as a Physician; because we were in need of compassion, he came as Savior.

Jerome

Lord, I have known the liberating power of your love,
*   just as I have known the suffocating weight of my need.*
You have come to me again and again in my distress,
*   and, when I thought there may be no way out,*
*   you led me to an open door.*
Today, I recount again, and in your presence,
*   some of those times when you "restored my fortunes."*
So that even as I call you,
*   I thank you.*

4

Wednesday of Advent I
PSALM 107

Then they cried out to the LORD *in their trouble,*
and he delivered them from their distress.
v. 6 *(13, 19, 28)*

P SALM 107, WHICH OPENS THE FIFTH AND FINAL "BOOK" of the complete Psalter, belongs to the type of psalms known as "historical" because it recounts events of God's saving intervention in the lives of his people. It is a story of God's deliverance. Indeed, it is four stories wrapped into one.

The opening call to "give thanks to the LORD" (1) is inspired by God's steadfast love, a love that not only "endures forever" but also shows itself in very specific divine acts. The psalmist illustrates the people of God being redeemed and gathered from the four compass points of the earth (3) with four examples of God's "wonderful works" (8).

1) vv. 4–9: Those who were lost in wilderness places cried out to the Lord as they wandered and fainted. God heard their cry, led them along clear pathways, and brought them safely to new dwelling places. They are to thank the Lord, for he fills the hungry with good things.

2) vv. 10–16: Those who were oppressed by darkness and despair, even held captive, by their own rebellious ways, cried out to God to deliver them from their distress. God brought them into the light of day, opening their eyes and shattering their chains. They are to thank the Lord, for he breaks the bonds that imprison them.

3) vv. 17–22: Those who were sick and suffering, whose maladies had brought them even to the point of death, cried out to God to save them. God sent forth his life-giving word, bringing healing and wholeness to those at the brink of destruction. They are to thank the Lord, tell of their deliverance, and sing for joy!

4) vv. 23–32: In the fourth and longest story (particularly loved by the seafaring world), those who "went down to the sea in ships" only to discover that their tiny vessels, no matter how grand while docked at port, were no match for the raging seas, cried to the Lord in their trouble. God stilled the storm that engulfed them, hushed the roaring winds, and brought the terrified voyagers—"at their wits' end" (27)—to a safe haven.

One can imagine the psalm being sung by a huge assembly in the temple as one voice proclaims each example of God's saving power, and answer is made by a chorus of cheers calling for thanksgiving and praise. The Jewish people would have surveyed their history and identified those occasions when these stories first took shape. As metaphors for our own histories, these same stories find reflection in our own lives without much effort—when we are lost, weighed down, sick, and tossed about by events or emotions beyond our control. At such times, says the psalmist, the wise person will pay attention to the work of God (43), finding evidence of the incarnate love of God there, even in the midst of troubles. Then the redeemed will add their own voice of thanksgiving for all the wonderful works of the Lord, and the song will be sung again.

FROM THE FATHERS

[Psalm 107] clearly proclaims the good news of the descent of God the Word from heaven . . . and the result of his coming. For it says, "He sent his Word and healed them." And we say distinctly that the Word of God was he who was sent as the Savior of all humankind . . . he healed and rescued them from their destruction. He did this simply by breaking what are called the gates of death and crushing the bars of iron.

Eusebius of Caesarea

> *Wandering . . . falling . . . lying down . . . reeling.*
> *These have all been among my conditions.*
> *Leading . . . raising . . . healing . . . saving.*
> *These have all been among your answers.*
> *When I cry to you, and when you answer,*
> *let me always remember . . . and give thanks.*

5

Thursday of Advent I
PSALM 97

The Lord reigns;
let the earth rejoice;
let the many coastlands be glad!

v. 1

SALM 97 IS ONE OF A GROUP SOMETIMES REFERRED TO as enthronement psalms, named for their use in celebrating not the coronation of a king but the sovereignty of Almighty God. These psalms serve as liturgical reminders that the supreme ruler of the universe—of all that is seen and all that is unseen—has never been nor ever can be dethroned by any other power, no matter how strong it might appear. Other enthronement psalms are 47, 93 (see below), 96, and 99. The psalmist perceives God's matchless strength in some of the most dramatic displays of nature—thunder and lightning, stormy seas, earthquakes, fire, floods, and winds. To the psalmist, these appearances (*theophanies*, or God showings) are not mere displays of raw power, like some kind of divine saber-rattling, devoid of meaning and purpose. They capture human attention and point their witnesses to the justice and righteousness of the Hand that is behind them. As well as awe, they call forth praise.

The psalmist sets forth three reasons to *rejoice* and *be glad:* God is matchless in his awe-inspiring power; God is just in governing all the earth; God is known by heaven and earth (and all the related powers) to be the only true God. Nothing has changed or ever will change about these truths, so the praises of God are always fitting, always timely. In other words, the praise of God is to be firmly founded upon only the changeless character of God, not the variable conditions of human circumstances.

According to this and other psalms, you don't need to be enjoying prosperity to praise the Lord. Good health, favorable circumstances, comfortable surroundings are not the criteria for rejoicing. The poet declares one unshakable and undeniable truth—the Lord is King. This is enough reason to be glad.

Of course, like many prophetic and poetic images in the Bible, Psalm 97 portrays a vision that, while true, is not yet fully evident. In a sense, the scene can only be viewed properly from heaven's eternal perspective, and that is precisely the psalmist's purpose. From our point of view, it appears that God's ways are frustrated by the world's injustices, his holiness is perverted by terrible things that are done in his name, and God's very existence is unrecognized, even denied by countless numbers of his own created sons and daughters.

Ultimately, however, none of these shadows, including the darkness in our own hearts and minds, can stand up to the radiant brilliance of the Lord. The day will come when the light of heaven will burst forth and bathe the world—and our hearts— in its splendor, when all the peoples will behold the glory of the Lord and give thanks for God's splendor. Until then, as we wait, we rejoice. Like the psalmist, we are glad for the things that, even now, we know to be true.

FROM THE FATHERS

Let us love, let us love freely and without any strings attached. It is God, after all, whom we love. We can find nothing better than God. Let us love him for his own sake, and ourselves and each other in him, but still for his sake. . . . "You that love the Lord, hate evil." . . . How can you love God, when you still love what God hates?

Augustine

Lighten my heart, today, Lord—
    Lighten it with a glimpse of your glory;
    Lighten it with a memory of your mercy;
    Lighten it with a hope for your blessing.
Lighten my heart, today, Lord—
    and for each of these things,
        I will give you thanks.

6

Friday of Advent I
PSALM 122

Our feet have been standing within your gates,
O Jerusalem!

v. 2

ND I SAW THE HOLY CITY, NEW JERUSALEM, COMING down out of heaven from God," wrote John the seer (Rev. 21:2). The completion of all human history and the fulfillment of all heaven's promises are contained within this radiant vision of the glorified Jerusalem. It is a far cry from the broken and conflicted city we see today. Perhaps Psalm 122 can remind us that, even as we pray for peace in the earthly city, we also join with Abraham, the father of faith, in looking "forward to the city which has foundations, whose builder and maker is God" (Heb. 11:10).

Of all the psalms called "Songs of Ascent"—the fifteen thought to have been used by worshipers as they made their pilgrimage ("going up") to Zion at a time of a Jewish festival—Psalm 122 seems to refer most directly to this practice, particularly from the point of view of one looking back upon a visit to the Holy City. It sounds as if the psalmist is reflecting on his experience, both with delight in the memory and with determination never to forget what he has seen.

The delight the psalmist feels is expressed in the first five verses, and it comes from the character of the city itself: Jerusalem is, above all else, the dwelling place of Yahweh, God's chosen habitation among the people he has called to be his own—"In Jerusalem will I put my name" (2 Kgs. 21:4). As such, the city embraces within its sacred walls both the "house of the LORD" (Ps. 122:1) and the "house of David" (5), a unifying of spiritual and temporal authority under one roof. This is where all the disparate tribes of Israel find their common lineage, their common purpose; and the psalmist delights with all his heart as he remembers standing upon such holy ground.

This vision inspires the pilgrim to make Jerusalem's future wellbeing a priority both in his prayers and in his intentions. In the closing half of the psalm, the writer seems to play on the name *Jerusalem* as he sings; *pray, peace, prosper, good*—these words each share a common connection with the Hebrew word that makes up part of *Jerusalem*: *shalom*. It is as if the city has now become part of him, and he part of it. The pilgrim returns to his own home even as he carries within his heart and upon his lips the name of a new home, *Jerusalem*.

"When I go and prepare a place for you," said Jesus to his disciples, "I will come again and will take you to myself, that where I am you may be also" (John 14:3). The goal of our life's pilgrimage is not a temporary visit to the home for which we were created, but a permanent stay in it. Until we arrive, it is good to sing Psalm 122 along the way.

FROM THE FATHERS

Here, "feet" is to be understood not as of the body but as of the soul. For how could a person on earth have his physical feet in heaven? Since Jerusalem, as Paul tells you, is in heaven, he also shows you how to stand in heaven when he says, "But our abode is in heaven" (Phil. 3:20)—the "abode" of your behavior, the "abode" of your deeds, the "abode" of your faith.

Ambrose

> *I don't think of heaven all that often, Lord,*
> > *but I do think about you.*
> *I want to be close to you, near you, with you.*
> *And where you are, certainly there is heaven also.*
> *So today, one foot on earth and one in heaven—*
> *That would be the best way for me to stand . . . and to walk.*

7

Saturday of Advent I
PSALM 51

Have mercy on me, O God,
according to thy steadfast love;
according to thy abundant mercy
blot out my transgressions.

v. 1

THE CONTEXT OF PSALM 51 IS GIVEN IN ITS superscription: "A Psalm of David, when Nathan the prophet came to him, after he had gone in to Bathsheba." The conversation between Nathan and David is recorded in 2 Samuel 12:1–13, and the story that led to the exchange is a familiar one (2 Sam. 11). Late one spring afternoon, the eyes—and then the hand—of King David falls lustfully upon Bathsheba, the wife of Uriah who was one of the kingdom's faithful soldiers. Bathsheba becomes pregnant with David's child and, in a desperate attempt to cover his own unfaithfulness, David deceitfully arranges for Uriah to be killed in battle. Then he takes Bathsheba to be his own wife.

With a remarkably pithy note of understatement, the record states that "the thing that David had done displeased the Lord." By God's revelation, David's secret villainy is brought into the light of day and Nathan the prophet is sent to confront him. Before heaven's court David is found inexcusably guilty of transgression. His sin looms before him like an unscalable mountain. He is helpless to overcome it. His soul is bereft at the very sight of it.

Four themes dominate David's repentance, and they are true of all repentance of sin. First, he has a deep sense of responsibility, of personal accountability for his choices and actions—*my* iniquity, *my* sin, *my* transgressions. Second, he knows that his sin against a neighbor was really sin against God—"against *you* have I sinned" (4). Third, with no recourse to his own worthiness, David's only appeal can be to the mercy of God—"according to your great compassion" (1, CEB). Finally, by that mercy, he can hope for and receive complete restoration from his sin—"let the bones you crushed rejoice once more" (8, CEB). Through forgiveness David can have unhindered fellowship with God once again.

Psalm 51 is one of seven psalms traditionally categorized as "penitential"—6, 32, 38, 51, 102, 130, 143—and for generations the church has put them to use in seasons that call for repentance and preparation. In each, the psalmist stands before God with the only "sacrifice" that can be offered, "a broken and contrite heart" (17). Such an offering, inspired by the convicting power of the Holy Spirit, is always acceptable to God. And it is always answered with mercy and forgiveness.

So it is that, a thousand years after David, Mercy's coming was announced to the world in the song of an old man who also knew the forgiveness of God. Filled with the Holy Spirit, Zechariah spoke of the divine calling of his son, John, to prepare the way of the Lord by offering God's people the forgiveness of their sins through the tender mercy of their God (Lk. 1:77–78). When the day dawned upon us from on high, David's prayer for mercy was answered for us all (Lk. 1:78–79).

FROM THE FATHERS

But how shall a person find grace with God? How else, except by lowliness of mind? For "God," James says, "resists the proud but gives grace to the humble" [James 4:6]; and "the sacrifice of God is a broken spirit, and a heart that is brought low God will not despise." For if humility is so lovely to human beings, it is much more so with God.

John Chrysostom

David's prayer says it all, Father.
There is nothing I can add—I can only make it my own.
And if I do, then let David's testimony be mine too
(as well as Zechariah's):
> *When he had fallen into sin, you raised him up again.*
With this psalm, I reach out my imploring hands to you,
> *and my own fallen heart.*

8

Second Sunday of Advent
PSALM 66

Come and hear, all you who fear God,
and I will tell what he has done for me.

v. 16

THE HEBREW INSCRIPTION OF THIS PSALM READS: "To the choirmaster—a song—a psalm." Most of the early Greek manuscripts (known as the Septuagint) add another word: *anastaseos*, meaning, "of the resurrection." This tells us that, by the second, or even late in the first century, Psalm 66 was probably sung by Christians at Easter, the feast of the Lord's resurrection.

Before Christians adopted Psalm 66 as a song in celebration of the resurrection, it was a song in celebration of God's deliverance of Israel. You hear in these words the prayer of a faithful Jew, coming to make his sacrifice in the temple, in gratitude to God for his saving deeds (3). On the one hand, those deeds took place generations ago, when the enslaved people of Israel were miraculously liberated from the fiery furnace of Egypt (Deut. 4:20) and brought through the Red Sea to a spacious land of promise and freedom (Ps. 66:11–12). But, to the psalmist, those "awesome deeds" had repeated in some way in his own personal life. "*I* was in trouble" (14), he says to any who will listen. "Come and hear, and I will tell you what the Lord has done for *me*" (16). To the psalmist, the delivering power of God is not something only from the distant past. The same God who turned the sea into dry land generations ago has kept the poet's feet from slipping in the mire today. Just as God heard the groaning of Israel under bondage (Ex. 2:23–24), "God has listened; he has given heed to the voice of my prayer" (Ps. 66:19), the psalmist sings.

For Christians, then, this psalm serves a similar purpose. In fourth-century Constantinople, John Chrysostom appointed it to be sung as the first antiphon at his divine liturgy for Easter. The Passover of the Israelites has become the Passover of Christ, which has become our own Passover from death to life. We can borrow the psalmist's words for our own every time we sing them. For we hear in them the words of our Savior, whose coming to bring victory over death and the grave has given us our own testimony:

You kept me among the living,

even when it seemed I would fall into the wasteland.

You tested me, O God,

smelted me in a furnace like silver.

It was as if you'd led me into a trap.

You laid an unbearable weight upon my back, and while I was bent over,

you allowed everyone to lord it over me.

I was burned in the fire and drowned in the water . . .

but you brought me back to life.

FROM THE FATHERS

Although the entrance is "straight and narrow," once inside we see a vast and limitless space, greater than any other anywhere. We have been told these things by eyewitnesses and heirs. They speak of their trials and distresses: "You have placed afflictions before us," but then they add, "You brought us out into a spacious place"—and, "You gave us space in our distress."

Athanasius

Father, you see the tight spot I am in.
The pressure seems to be coming from every direction . . .
> *mostly from the inside.*
>> *It feels as though I can hardly move.*
You tell me that the grave-cloth that binds me today
> *will tomorrow become the white robe of praise.*
In the meantime, hear my prayer,
> *and do not leave me alone.*

9

Monday of Advent II
PSALM 34

I will bless the LORD *at all times;*
his praise shall continually be in my mouth.

v. 1

T HE PSALMIST'S JOY IS SO FULL THAT HE IS DETERMINED to do two things: praise God at all times, and get as many others as possible to join in. Then, once he has the attention of his listeners, he invites them to live their entire lives to the glory of God.

The poet begins: "I will bless the LORD at *all* times," the Lord's "praise shall *continually* be in my mouth." The praise of God should never cease, because the love of God never ceases. Nothing weakens in God's commitment to bless his people; should anything weaken in their whole-hearted gratitude for his kindness?

The superscription of the psalm ("A psalm of David, when he feigned madness before Abimelech, so that he drove him out, and he went away") refers to events recorded in 1 Samuel 21:10–22:2. Fleeing from Saul, the young David futilely seeks refuge in the Philistine city of Gath, from which he narrowly escapes after pretending to be insane. He hides out in a cave, where he is joined by upwards of four hundred equally desperate friends and family. The psalm title seems to indicate it may have been composed and sung in the presence of David's fellow fugitives.

The opening half of the psalm contains the psalmist's personal testimony to the goodness of God (1–11). He recounts the wonderful ways that God has already heard and answered him when he was in trouble: I sought and God answered; I cried and God heard; I feared and God delivered. The psalmist cannot say enough about how faithfully and repeatedly God has come to his rescue. It is a natural step then, to rally everyone around him to join in giving thanks.

He summons them to more than sharing a joyful song, however. Praise offered in the temple or a synagogue (or a cave), if genuine, can come only from genuine righteousness lived in the home and among neighbors. The second half of the psalm contains the psalmist's succinct description of a *life* that is full of praise: telling the truth, doing good, seeking peace (12–22).

In his letter to the Ephesians, the apostle Paul writes that all who have put their hope in Christ have been "destined and appointed to live for the praise of his glory" (Eph. 1:12). Both the Old and New Testaments teach that the praise of God is best expressed through the lives, not only the lips, of God's people. Pursuing what is good, standing against what is evil, speaking what is true, humbling the heart, trusting in the Lord— these are the ways to praise and thank the Lord "at all times."

FROM THE FATHERS

The Lord loves thankful people. They never cease to praise him, and they regularly thank him. In both good times and bad times they offer praise and thanksgiving to God. They worship the Lord, the God of *all* times, without regard to what the times are like.

Athanasius

Father, if I offer the kindling—just a few sticks and a bit of brush—
Will you help me set a fire of praise in my heart?
One tongue of flame is all I need.
And all you need is something to burn.
So today I bring the twigs of my thoughts, my decisions, my desires,
And the great logs of your great deeds in my life.
I'm ready, Lord.
Let's make a fire of praise!

10

Tuesday of Advent II
PSALM 149

Let Israel be glad in his Maker;
let the sons of Zion rejoice in their King.

v. 2

ESPECIALLY IN OUR TIME, PSALM 149'S MILITANT TONE when calling for all the faithful to praise God should not be mistaken for a call to war. On the spiritual battlefield, however, praise of God is among the most effective weapons—it actually bears the power of God. The book of Nehemiah describes a scene in the rebuilding of the temple after the exile: "Those who carried burdens were laden in such a way that each with one hand labored on the work and with the other held his weapon" (4:17). The work of building a house of prayer went hand in hand with the work of defending it. Sword and shovel each had its place.

Something similar is going on with Psalm 149. "Let the praise of God be in their mouths and a double-edged sword in their hands," writes the psalmist (6, NIV). Surely he is talking about something more than a literal weapon of war. At other points in the Bible, the metaphorical image of a sharp sword is used to indicate the incisive truth of the Word of God (see Isa. 49:2; Ps. 45:2–3). The visionary of Revelation pictures the One who is called "Faithful and True" finally returning to govern the whole earth with a sharp sword issuing forth from his mouth, "with which to strike down the nations" (Rev. 19:15). He who came first in a manger will come then on a throne, bearing the Almighty name "King of kings and Lord of lords" (16).

Like the seer of the apocalypse, the psalmist is looking toward that day when all earthly powers and authorities will bow in adoration (willingly or unwillingly) before the true Sovereign of all. Then, no nation nor people, no ruler nor noble, will be able to stand upright before the Lord's coming. Until that day, however, it is for the saints to sing, to rejoice, to dance, to play the timbrel and harp, to be joyful in the glory of God. This makes every act of praise a declaration of truth: the Lord God reigns, forever and ever.

FROM THE FATHERS

"Sing to the Lord a new song." "Well, I am singing," you say. Yes, you are singing. Of course you are singing. I can hear you. But do not let your life give evidence against your tongue. Sing with your voices, sing also with your hearts; sing with your mouths, sing also with your conduct. . . . Do you want to sing God his praises? Be yourselves what you sing.   *Augustine*

> *Lord, you invite me to sing your praises.*
> *Not just to think them, but to sing them.*
> *You want my voice as well as my heart.*
> *Apparently it's not enough just to whisper.*
> *You want real sound.*
> *So, real sound I will give you.*

1 1

Wednesday of Advent II
PSALM 57

Be exalted, O God, above the heavens!
Let thy glory be over all the earth!
vv. 5, 11

I S PSALM 57 A PRAYER OF LAMENT OR A SONG OF PRAISE?
It is both, really, but praise is given the last word.

The psalmist uses vivid imagery to describe his predicament as well as the power of God to save him. For example,
his cry for mercy and help is made as he hides himself "in the
shadow of [God's] wings" (1). This is an almost technical
reference to the golden wings of the cherubim that hover over
the ark of the covenant in the temple (Ex. 25:18–20; 1 Kgs.
6:27–28), but the Hebrew could also refer to the shadow of
"your *Shekinah*," meaning the glory of God's presence. *Shekinah*
is sometimes used to speak of the pillars of cloud and fire that
guided and protected the children of Israel during their sojourn
in the wilderness (see Ex. 13:20–22).

In either case, even while troubled and in danger, the
psalmist pictures himself securely concealed in the protective
shade of God's presence. He may be hiding in a cave (see the

opening ascription), but he sees himself resting under the cover of God's merciful and limitless power. In this sense, he is in truth surrounded by heaven's glorious light, even as dark shadows loom over his head.

The psalmist pictures his enemies vividly (1, 4, 6). They are like a violent storm that leaves nothing but destruction in its wake. They are like ravenous lions, stealthily stalking their prey, with teeth as long as spears and as sharp as arrows, and with pointed swords for tongues. They are like hunters, skillfully laying their snares and digging their traps. Pursued by such cruel forces and foes, how can the psalmist hope to escape?

Twice in the psalm a refrain of victory is repeated: "Be exalted, O God, above the heavens! Let thy glory be over all the earth!" (5, 11). God, the Lord of the universe, reigns over heaven above—where the storms of destruction are carried on the winds; the glory of God fills the earth below—where prowling enemies hunt and scheme. The psalmist's vision of God—in glory, exaltation, faithfulness, and love—dispels his vision of danger. And that God-given vision inspires his fearful heart to awaken with praise and thanksgiving. For hundreds of years, some liturgical traditions have assigned Psalm 57 to be a regular part of morning prayer. The reason is clear: the night visions are past; the darkness gives way to dawn, fear dissolves with the rising Sun. Praise is the only fit greeting to give the new day.

FROM THE FATHERS

You are exalted, you who were enclosed in your mother's womb; you who were made in her whom you had made; you who lay in the manger; you, suckled at the breast as a baby, according to the very nature of flesh; you holding up the world and being held by your mother; . . . you, who were hungry for our sakes, thirsty for our sakes, tired along the road for our sakes; . . . you, arrested, bound, scourged, crowned with thorns, hung on the tree, pierced with the lance, you dead, you buried: "Be exalted above the heavens, O God!"

Augustine

O God, my Creator and Redeemer,
> *whose glory and love fill the universe,*
> *whose power and mercy cover the whole earth:*
Give light to my eyes,
> *that, where now I can see only darkness, I may see you.*
And give light to my heart,
> *that, where now I can only fear, I may praise you. Amen.*

12

Thursday of Advent II
PSALM 40

*I have told the glad news of deliverance
in the great congregation.*

v. 9

I WAITED, AND I WAITED, AND I WAITED," MIGHT be the opening words of this prayer—or, rather, this testimony. It is as if the psalmist is standing up before an assembly of fellow worshipers and telling them the story of his deliverance which, he admits quite frankly, did not come as quickly as he first wanted. As someone has said, God is never late, which means that waiting is bringing us into line with his divine timetable.

At the right time, God did answer the psalmist's cry for help. He reached down from heaven and, with arms strong enough to carry the freight of the whole universe, snatched his servant's soul out of the crushing grip of the quagmire. We are not told the exact circumstances of the psalmist's trapped condition, but we can look to our own experience of sufferings and difficulties with destructive holds upon us too strong to bear, much less escape. "For the LORD has ransomed Jacob," wrote the prophet Jeremiah, "and has redeemed him *from hands too strong for him*" (Jer. 31:11). We come to

know God's profound deliverance when we are at our most helpless. Psalm 40, therefore, begins as a "new song" of thanksgiving
to God, whose saving works are too numerous to be counted and
whose strength is the only hope of our salvation.

The writer to the Hebrews sees in this psalm the testimony
of Jesus, whose singular delight was to do the will of his Father
(Heb. 10:5–10). He declared to the world the utter reliability of
God, and then endured suffering at the hands of that same world,
all the while remaining steadfast in his determination to "trust in
the Lord."

Within a few verses the psalmist turns from addressing the
people to addressing God. His testimony of recent deliverance—"I
have not concealed thy steadfast love and thy faithfulness from
the great congregation" (Ps. 40:10)—becomes the very foundation of a renewed plea for God's help: "Do not thou, O LORD,
withhold thy mercy from me" (11). Clearly, he is in trouble again
(how familiar his story is to us). This time his own sins have taken
him by the throat (12) and, as if to add insult to injury, others
seek to do him harm as well (14). But, he knows where to turn in
his need, and in whom to place his hope. "*I* am poor and needy,"
he cries. "*Thou* art my help and my deliverer" (17). He has waited
upon the Lord before and he will wait again. Still, like all of us,
he'd like not to wait too long and cannot help adding, "Do not
tarry, O my God."

FROM THE FATHERS

Christ has heard the prayer of his servants and has brought us out from the pit of misery and from the mire of dregs. We were drowning there, trapped in the whirlpool of our sins. Our soul was powerless to save itself. . . . Thanks be to the Lord Jesus, God's only Son, who came down from heaven to forgive us our sins—to save us from the pit and slime of this world, from the mud and mire of this earth, from this body doomed to death. In his own flesh he has restored our soul and steadied our tottering footsteps. Strengthened by God's Word and absolved through the cross of our Lord, we walk no longer in the shame and disfigurement of vice, but in the forgiveness of sin, rooted and built in Christ. . . . May that rock, which follows those who thirst, confirm the weak and unsteady, and may that firm foundation never be wanting to those in danger of falling.

Ambrose

Yes, Lord, thank you! Many, many times, thank you!
You heard my cry, reached from heaven, and snatched me up.
May my new song today be a new thank you!

13

Friday of Advent II
PSALM 56

Nevertheless, though I am sometime afraid,
yet put I my trust in thee.
v. 3 (BCP)

THE ANCIENT EDITORS OF THE PSALMS ASSIGNED
Psalm 56 to David. Its superscription, "A Miktam of
David, when the Philistines seized him in Gath," refers
again to those events recorded in 1 Samuel 21 and 22, when,
fleeing before Saul, David pretended to be crazy and took refuge
among his mortal enemies, the Philistines. *Out of the frying pan
and into the fire,* you might say about David's predicament. The
psalmist puts it more directly: "My enemies trample upon me
all day long, for many fight against me proudly" (2).

The prayer is essentially divided into two parts—verses
1–3 and verses 5–9—with a similar refrain concluding each
part in 4 and 10–11. The last two verses of the psalm sum up
the writer's vow to go on giving thanks to God for keeping him
safe. Verses 1–3 describe a desperate situation from which the
psalmist can see no escape. His enemies prevail over him and
he appears to be at their mercy. The most fundamental human

emotion rises up within him under these circumstances—the same emotion that grips us all when danger threatens—he is afraid.

The psalmist further describes and laments his perilous situation (5–7), but not before introducing a new thought that makes all the difference in the world. To do so he begins with "Nevertheless" (3, BCP). A *nevertheless* we utter in the midst of our fear is like a door handle that opens the way into a room with a different view—*God's* view—of the reality around us.

This *nevertheless* is like the first word of the last chapter of Luke's Gospel. For many paragraphs, Luke has been describing the betrayal, the trial, the suffering, and finally the death of Christ. As he opens a new door by introducing the story of the Resurrection, however, he begins: *"But, on the first day of the week, at early dawn"* (Lk. 24:1). The *nevertheless* of the psalmist's prayer, like the Evangelist's *but*, introduces a declaration that there is more to the story—much, much more. "I *am* afraid," admits David, "*nevertheless*, I will put my trust in God" (3, 11, BCP). Why? Because God's word, God's faithfulness, God's mercy will prevail. He who counts and records every fearful tear shed in the darkness (this is not surprising since he also knows every hair of our head) will in the end make it possible for me to walk fearlessly in the light. The shadows are sure to come, *nevertheless*. . . .

FROM THE FATHERS
[In this psalm] the holy church is describing what she suffers in this world, for we know that she endures struggles with the devil

without any relief. . . . Our enemy does not weary of toil, nor does he at any time depart when overcome. He returns all the more oppressively if by divine grace we have been able to conquer him. . . . So let none of the faithful complain that he is troubled by the incessant wiles of the devil, for if we wish to belong to Christ, we must always endure the enmity of the devil in this life.

Cassiodorus

Once again I put my trust in you, Lord,
to be my defender, my protector, my victor, my Savior.

14

Saturday of Advent II
PSALM 61

*Lead thou me
to the rock that is higher than I.*

v. 2

THE PSALMIST IS DISTRAUGHT, AND IT APPEARS THAT what weighs upon his heart is the overwhelming sense of distance he feels between himself and God. "From the ends of the earth will I call upon thee," he cries (2, BCP). His sense of dejection is not unfamiliar. "Where is God?" we ask miserably, when God's ways are dark and our days seem devoid of his presence. At the end of our tether we are quick to feel that God has removed himself from us, that he stands at a distance, that perhaps he has even forgotten us. Psalm 61 is a prayer for just such an occasion.

If this is in fact a prayer of David the king (see verse 6), there must have been many times he felt alone under the weight of his office—as there would be for any leader. The clouds of duty and responsibility, the storms of conflict and even war must have obscured the brightness of God's presence. Nevertheless, the king knew where to turn—to *whom* to turn—in such times. When his own strength was depleted, when all hopeful vision and strength of will failed, the psalmist—like all of us—cried. He shed his tears before the Lord. In a few succinct phrases, he likens God to a high rock upon which he can stand, a tower in which he can find refuge, a tent in which he can dwell in safety, and wings under which he can find covering (2–4). Any one of these images can give consolation to a fearful heart. Put together, they describe a God strong enough and present enough to help the king under any circumstances.

Once the psalmist makes his petition, he can make his promise. Despite how he feels, he knows that he is not alone. He knows God is ever-present to help and to hide him. Therefore he says with a newfound confidence that he will live before God forever, singing praise to God's name, and that he will fulfill his vows (probably referring to his coronation).

Being devoid of personal strength, he can rely on the strength of God and recommit himself to God's service. Even as he looks for God's steadfast love to be his help, he promises his own steadfast commitment to be God's servant (7–8). In Psalm 61, renewed dedication accompanies fervent intercession.

FROM THE FATHERS

[The Lord] says, "I shall build my church on this rock, and the gates of the lower world shall not prevail against it" (Matt. 16:18). Although the gates of the devil strike against it, yet they do not overthrow Christ's church; although the flood of faithlessness inundates it, it does not undermine the house of faith. For [the church] is able to say truthfully to its helper, "When my heart was disquieted, you raised me up on a rock."

Bede

My faith is anything but rock-solid, Lord.
My hope is equally fickle.
And my love is probably the least reliable thing of all.
Rock of all the ages
    —of all my ages—
Fix my faith and my hope and my love
    on Thee.

15

Third Sunday of Advent
PSALM 84

My soul longs, yea faints for the courts of the LORD;
my heart and flesh sing for joy to the living God.

v. 2

HOW *LOVELY* IS THY DWELLING PLACE, O LORD OF HOSTS" (Ps. 84:1). The Hebrew term, *yedidot* (from the verb *dwd*, which also forms the name David) carries a stronger meaning than *pleasing*. Elsewhere in the Bible, the word always refers to those "beloved" by someone, particularly by God. So, the psalmist is saying he is in love with God's house. Why this deep affection and desire? Nowhere does the poet speak of how the temple looks, or of the manifold liturgical activities that take place there. His longing for "the courts of the Lord" is inspired not by the beauty of objects and activities but by the beauty of the One who lives there—"my heart and my flesh rejoice in the living God" (2, BCP). For this reason, he utters three benedictions upon the one who makes his pilgrimage to Zion.

Blessed are those who dwell in your house (4, ESV). If making a pilgrimage to the temple is an occasion of great joy and celebration, how much happier would the person be who lived there all the time? Like the birds of the air that nest in the rafters of the tabernacle, such a person might make his permanent home within the presence of God. There he could sing unceasing praises to the Lord God of hosts. No more would desire and longing define his days. Fulfillment would replace restlessness, and—even by only standing at the door (10)—contentment would be his forever.

Blessed are those whose strength is in you (5, ESV). The psalmist knows that a pilgrimage to Jerusalem can be a dangerous undertaking, but those who draw upon God are sure to arrive safely (7). The man who loves God's house, whose well of strength is God himself, is not afraid of even the driest valleys. The landscape of our soul's pilgrimage is often marked with rough and parched terrain, but the one who walks with God will never fail to find (even make) a stream out of the desert (6). (See Isaiah 35:6.)

Blessed is the one who trusts in you (12, ESV). This is the heart of the psalmist's benedictions. God is the "light and defence" (BCP; RSV: the "sun and shield") of them that live according to his ways. Nothing good is withheld from them, for God himself is the sum of their longing.

FROM THE FATHERS

Somebody may ask, "Why in the valley of tears, in the place that God has set for the contest—or for the conflict—why has he placed us as athletes? Why has he willed us to fight?" The psalmist gives the answer: He has willed that this place be set for us as an arena that he may reward our victory with a crown. . . . "They go from strength to strength"; hence, unless we are strong here, we cannot have greater strength there. . . . Do you want to be a person of fortitude there? Then be one here first. Do you want to be crowned there? Fight here.

Jerome

> *My strength is in you, Lord.*
> *Today, even in my weakness—especially in my weakness,*
>   *I am strong.*
> *So, if the fight comes to me today, Lord,*
>   *I will fight on your side . . . by your side.*

16

Monday of Advent III
PSALM 6

Be gracious to me, O LORD, *for I am languishing;*
O LORD, *heal me.*

v. 2

FOR SOMEONE WHO LIVES WITH GOD, WHAT IS THE appropriate response to trouble? Whether from inward distress of soul, or from outward distress by adversity? The psalms teach us that the proper response is always *prayer*. Through prayers, the psalmists bring forward every manner of suffering. There is no affliction that is not suitable grist for the mill of conversation with God.

In the case of Psalm 6, affliction has taken hold in both the body and the soul of the psalmist. "My bones are *in agony*," says one translation, and "my soul is in *deep anguish*" (2–3, NIV). In both cases, the Hebrew word may be translated literally as "terrified." His condition is one of utmost panic, physically as well as emotionally. "Shaking with terror," says the NRSV. Moreover, while he is fearfully aware that his enemies (be they physical or spiritual) seek his destruction, he is most dreadfully afraid that his chief enemy may be the Lord himself—"O LORD, rebuke me not in *thy* anger" (1).

The psalmist has a conscience, and before God he knows that he stands unworthy. Were he to die with his thoughts, words, and deeds left unabsolved, he would be banished to death as an unreconciled enemy of the Lord. This is a prospect he cannot bear, and so tears of grief and despair soak his pillow night after night.

However, fear does not have the final say. The psalmist has brought his complaint to the "throne of grace," where he "may receive mercy and find grace to help in time of need" (Heb. 4:16). There is a distinct change in the tone of the psalm after verse 7. "The LORD has heard my supplication," he declares (9). The sound of his weeping does not go unnoticed by the Lord. The psalmist is left neither alone in his despair, nor without hope for deliverance.

The tide has turned at last, and it will be his enemies, not his own soul and body, who will be "sorely troubled" (10). What if the psalmist had not turned to the Lord in his desperation? As pitiful as was his condition, his voice was a welcome sound to the ears of heaven. The psalmist's panic is replaced by a renewed confidence that God has heard and accepted his prayer (9). A thousand years later, the apostle Paul put it succinctly to his readers: "If God is for us, who can be against us?" (Rom. 8:31, ESV).

FROM THE FATHERS

[The psalmist] constantly invokes this word *Lord*, as though adducing some claim to pardon and grace. This, after all, is our greatest hope, his loving-kindness beyond telling, and the fact that he is such a one as to be ready to pardon.

John Chrysostom

Father, there is no question that my sin causes me much pain,
    in my bones, and in my soul.
And you are the great Physician of both.
Heal me, Lord—
Relieve the pain.
Forgive the sin.
Save my whole life.

17

Tuesday of Advent III
PSALM 25

Make me to know thy ways, O LORD;
teach me thy paths.
Lead me in thy truth, and teach me.

vv. 4–5

S OME PSALMS MAKE USE OF A POETIC DEVICE KNOWN AS an acrostic. Psalm 25 is one of these. Each of its twenty-two verses begins with a successive letter of the Hebrew alphabet. (Others are Psalms 9, 10, 34, 37, 111, 112, 119, and 145.) Psalm 25 takes this one step further. The opening letters of the beginning verse, the middle verse, and the last verse spell out the Hebrew root for *teach* or *learn* (alaph), which in fact summarizes the content of the psalm. "Show me thy ways, O LORD, and teach me thy paths" (Ps. 25:3, BCP). This psalmist, who is apparently experienced in the ways of God's mercy ("remember not the sins of my youth"), requests God's guidance in the midst of his troubles, even as his enemies threaten to destroy him. This is a prayer for instruction and direction that can be useful in any situation.

As in so many of the psalms of lament, the psalmist holds up his soul before God in search of assistance. The image is rich with feeling, as if the psalmist has succeeded in reaching down within himself, taking his inquiring heart within his own feeble hands, and raising it before his Lord and Maker: "To thee, O LORD, I lift up my soul" (1).

In a time of trouble, rather than answering back to his adversaries, or acting vengefully on his own behalf, the psalmist exercises his faith and turns his aching soul to the Lord. "Let me not be ashamed," he prays (2, KJV). He is asking that the faith he puts in God not be placed in vain. By answering, God will sustain the psalmist's faith and show to his enemies that such faith is not misplaced. No sooner does he make this plea for deliverance, however, than the psalmist prays for guidance: "Show me your ways" (4, NIV). With this petition, the psalmist puts legs on his trust in God. For faith in God's power is empty if not accompanied by obedience to God's ways.

Certainly, the psalmist is mindful of the mercy and grace of God. He remembers them "from of old" (6) and he is counting on them now in order to be delivered from his troubles. But his trust is not passive. With his eyes "ever toward the LORD" (15) he expects not only deliverance but also counsel. The psalmist looks for the hand of God so that he might do the will of God.

FROM THE FATHERS

[God] will teach his ways not to those who want to run on ahead, as if they could rule themselves better than he can, but to those who do not strut about with their heads in the air or dig in their heels, when his easy yoke and light burden are set on them.

Augustine

Lord, what more could I ask than to have you as my Teacher?
Because you are my Creator, you know me through and through.
Because you are my Lord, there is nothing beyond your wisdom.
Because you are my Savior, you will always help me in my weakness.
What better Teacher could I ever desire?

18

Wednesday of Advent III
PSALM 103

Bless the LORD, *O my soul,*
and forget not all his benefits.

v. 2

SALM 103 BEGINS AND ENDS WITH THE EXACT SAME phrase: "Bless the LORD, O my soul!" The repeated phrase is like two bookends that sum up all that is contained in a long shelf of texts and manuscripts that stand between them. This is a call to worship rooted in specific events and experiences of God's blessings.

Counting one's blessings: Psalm 103 conveys the depth of meaning contained in this very ordinary and often overlooked spiritual exercise. Dietrich Bonhoeffer once reminded his readers that, in times of difficulty, when we are tempted to give in to our worst inclinations, the enemy of our souls has only one goal in mind: "Satan does not here fill us with hatred of God, but with forgetfulness of God."[1] The path to renewed faith and joy often leads through the memory, and if there is a central theme to Psalm 103 it is this: *remember.*

It seems that the psalmist has had some kind of personal experience of God's mercy and healing and, as he calls to mind the love he has received, his gratitude overflows into song. He invokes everything in his being to praise the One who has saved him. But this is not enough. The author is but one person in the midst of a whole people who have experienced the compassion and goodness of God. His compelling instruction to "forget not all [God's] benefits" (2) is meant for them as well. In fact, it is meant for all of humanity, for all those whose very breath is a sign of the kindness of their Creator. By the end of the psalm, "all that is within *me*" (1) expands to "in all *places of his dominion*" (22). There is not a single corner within the human soul nor within the vast domain of creation that has not known, and therefore should not remember, the "steadfast love of the LORD" (17).

The human memory is both fickle and selective. Too often it is the unjust and hurtful experiences that linger longest in our minds, taking up valuable space in our memory that could otherwise be occupied with thoughts of God and of his blessings. As if to drive away these interlopers, the psalmist sounds almost urgent as he recounts the innumerable ways in which God shows his care: forgiving sin, healing sickness, saving from destruction, satisfying need, renewing strength. Call to mind the mercy of God, insists Psalm 103. In other words, *remember the God who remembers you*.

FROM THE FATHERS

What, I ask, do we think cannot be forgiven us when the Lord forgives all our iniquities? Or what do we think cannot be healed in us, when the Lord heals all our diseases? . . . Therefore, let no one despairing of the physician remain in his infirmity; let no one, downplaying the mercy of God, waste away in iniquities. The apostle calls out that "Christ died for the ungodly" [Rom. 5:6].

Fulgentius of Ruspe

Today, Father, I call to mind these blessings from your hand:
For each of them, I bless you,
    and praise you,
    and thank you.
And I hold them in my heart—like sentinels of truth—
    to be called upon at any moment,
      to remind me of your goodness
      and to lead me to praise once again.

19

Thursday of Advent III
PSALM 8

When I look at thy heavens, the work of thy fingers . . .
what is man that thou art mindful of him,
and the son of man, that thou dost care for him?
vv. 3—4

WHO HAS STOOD IN SILENCE UNDER THE LUMINOUS canopy of a midnight sky and not wondered at the mysteries contained in this vast universe? No sooner is the question formed in our minds—"How far can my gaze reach into this never-ending vastness?"—than the boundless measure of the answer provokes in us an overwhelming sense of our own tininess. The psalmist (unlike us, the inhabitants of the electric light bulb age) probably looked upon the nighttime sky every evening. On one occasion, the questions evoked by the starry vision took shape in a poem, and that poem eventually became a hymn to be sung in the house of God, where it is still sung today.

In his letter to the Romans, Paul writes that the invisible nature of God is clearly visible in all the things that God has made (Rom. 1:19–20). If we will pay attention, the book of creation will tell us a good deal about its Author. The psalmist's contemplation of heaven inspired him to "see" beyond the stars and to give praise to their Creator—to *his* Creator. Even as the psalmist "considers the heavens," his thoughts descend back to earth. Given the infinite scope of God's handiwork, he wonders, where does humanity fit in? Who are we, mere specks, that you not only see us, but care about us? (Ps. 8:4).

A clue to the answer is given even before the question is asked. Standing under the glorious night sky, the psalmist reflects that the infinite God's praises are "chanted" in the squeals and cries of infants and children (2). This poetic visionary sees in the middle of the night what an exhausted parent can hardly imagine—an intimate and wondrous connection between God's uncontainable glory and the blubbering of a newborn babe.

The psalmist is struck by the inscrutable paradox: within all creation, human life seems hardly noticeable, almost inconsequential, but in the thoughts of the Creator, human life is immeasurably valuable, dignified, and noble. "So God created man in his own image, in the image of God he created him; male and female he created them. And God blessed them" (Gen. 1:27–28). Even this thought humbles the writer and leads him, once again, to give praise to God. The ancient poet does the modern reader a profound favor by sharing his nocturnal prayer with us. From time to time we would do well to stand with him under the stars, lift our own eyes toward heaven, and hear what prayer the vision might inspire.

FROM THE FATHERS

"What is man that you are mindful of him?" What is this new mystery concerning me? I am small and great, lowly and exalted, mortal and immortal, earthly and heavenly. I am connected with the world below, and likewise with God; I am connected with the flesh, and likewise with the spirit. I must be buried with Christ, rise with Christ, be joint heir with Christ.

Gregory of Nazianzus

I don't understand why you think so much of me, Lord.
When I consider what you have done for me,
> *when I take the time to number the stars of your mercy to me,*
>> *I am left in awe at the loving attention you have given me.*
Can you help my heart to be filled with more awe than anxiety,
> *more gratitude than grief,*
> *more wonder than worry?*
Then, like the psalmist, I can sit amazed at your goodness,
> *And, with the mouth of a child,*
> *I can chant your glory.*

20

Friday of Advent III
PSALM 32

Blessed is he whose transgression is forgiven,
whose sin is covered.

v. 1

THERE ARE TWO BASIC MESSAGES TO PSALM 32: when we depart from the ways of God, confession of sin is the pathway to pardon; and, God will surely lead us in those ways if we will follow. The first message has to do with the joy of forgiveness, in this case, of *being* forgiven. The second message has to do with God's willingness, even God's desire, to forgive our wandering ways and to then keep his eye upon us. Living in the light of these unalterable truths makes the psalmist truly blessed.

The most famous description of the requirements for a blessed life is the Sermon on the Mount. There Jesus lists nine conditions for true, lasting happiness and fullness of life, each beginning, "Blessed are the . . ." (see Matt. 5:1–11). The Hebrew word translated as *blessed*, used here and elsewhere by the psalmist, basically means "happy." But it has less to do with an emotion than with the spiritual condition of the person who pursues God's ways—who actually participates in life with God. Thus it is that *blessed* serves as the opening word of the entire Psalter: "Blessed is the man who walks not in the counsel of the wicked, nor stands in the way of sinners, nor sits in the seat of scoffers; but his delight is in the law of the LORD, and on his law he meditates day and night. He is like a tree planted by streams of water, that yields its fruit in its season, and its leaf does not wither. In all that he does, he prospers" (Ps. 1:1–3).

In contrast to this state of ceaseless prosperity, the condition of the person who tries to hide his sin is one of arid misery. The psalmist describes himself under such circumstances as a scorched plant withering under the hot summer sun. There are no flowing streams of water for the unrepentant. Releasing the spring, the source of all refreshment and revival, requires that the psalmist admit his wrong before God. Blessedness really is only a prayer away: "I acknowledged my sin to you . . . and you forgave the guilt of my sin."

Once he has turned around, admitting both to himself and to God that he has been wrong, the psalmist is relieved of the heaviness of heart that has been weighing him down. Now, if he will obediently give himself to God's instruction, he can walk freely with his Lord, to be led, without "bit and bridle" (9), in the ways of peace and gladness.

FROM THE FATHERS

When you see people being baptized and ransomed out of a generation that is perishing, and you are in wonder at the loving-kindness of God toward the human race, then sing to them Psalm 32.

Athanasius

Father, if your forgiving love were not enough to erase my sin,
　　then I would in fact be lost,
　　　and without hope.
But, if your grace is sufficient,
And your Son's work is finished,
And your steadfast love never comes to an end,
　　then I am in fact found,
　　　and without despair.

21

Saturday of Advent III
PSALMS 42 & 43

Hope in God;
for I shall again praise him,
my help and my God.
v. 5

IN SEVERAL HEBREW MANUSCRIPTS, THESE TWO PSALMS
are joined together, which indicates that at one time they
probably were a single psalm. The fact that they share a
common refrain—"Why are you cast down, O my soul" (see Ps.
42:6, 11, and 43:5)—is strong support for this view. The song is
the prayer of someone who is experiencing an excruciating sense
of separation from God. The psalmist uses poignant imagery: *Just
as a thirsty deer pants after a flowing stream, so my dry soul craves after
the life-giving drink that comes from your presence, O Lord* (42:1). While
the Hebrew word *nephesh* is translated here and elsewhere in the
psalms as *soul*, meaning a person's most true *self*, it can also mean
throat. The psalmist's longing for God is virtually audible, like the
croaking sound of a parched throat. The psalmist is looking for
more than refreshment—he is thirsting for life itself. Water—that
most basic of life-giving elements: remove it from our reach for

only a few days and we are consigned to a bitter and uncomfortable death.

So, what is the condition of a dehydrated soul? While the sweet waters of God's presence are absent, the psalmist has not run dry of his own salty tears. They are the only moisture he has known for days. What makes it worse is that those who see his condition, rather than offering comfort, add scorn to his own doubts. "Now where is this God of yours?" they cruelly sneer. The bitterness of the present makes this tormented soul nostalgic for the time when he went joyfully to the temple with his fellow worshipers. In fact, he was often the first of the whole assembly to go into the house of the Lord with praise on his lips. He remembers the "good ol' days" and he mourns their loss. Where have those days gone? As only a poet can say it, he is afraid he will die of thirst for God, and at the same time fears he will drown in a sea of sorrow. *All your waves and stormy seas have flooded over me* (7). Like Peter sinking into the roiling waters of the Galilee, the psalmist has only one cry to make: "Lord, save me!" (Matt. 14:30, NIV).

In the end, after pouring out his bitter complaint, it is almost as if the psalmist is having a word with himself. He knows from experience that God can and *will* save him. *Soul,* he says, *why have you given up hope? (Hang on just a little longer, dry throat!) Trust your God, and before long your thirst will be quenched and, once again, you will be singing.*

FROM THE FATHERS

In God's home there is an everlasting party. What is celebrated there is not some occasion that passes; the choirs of angels keep eternal festival, for the eternally present face of God is joy never diminished. This is a feast day that does not open at dawn, or close at sundown.

Augustine

> I thirst for many things, Lord,
> > but not enough for you.
> Yet what is this dryness in my soul,
> > if not the unquenched desire to know you?
> Today, I'd like it if drinking from you
> > lasted longer than my drinking from anything else,
> > > if only by a drop or two.

22

Fourth Sunday of Advent
PSALM 89

I will sing of thy steadfast love, O LORD, for ever;
with my mouth I will proclaim thy faithfulness to all generations.

v. 1

isericordias Domini in aeternum cantabo—THE OPENING words of Psalm 89, as they are sung in Latin (I will sing of your steadfast love, O Lord, forever)—appear on a banner issuing from the mouth of Teresa of Avila in a famous portrait done of the saint in 1576, while she was still living. The painting portrays the elderly Teresa being visited by the Holy Spirit who descends in the form of a dove, a vision she had on the eve of Pentecost. With these words taken from the psalm, the artist expresses the theme of St. Teresa's life: her continued response of praise to God through all the varied experiences of her life. And praising God for his "steadfast love and faithfulness" in all circumstances—including the most chaotic—is precisely the message of Psalm 89.

The fifty-two-verse psalm can be divided into three parts. Part 1 (1–18) is a declaration of God's sovereign rule over all creation, praising him for his faithfulness, which "is firm as the heavens" (Ps.

89:2). The universe is marked with countless signs of God's loving care. Its grandeur and order reflect the very nature of its Creator— great, awesome, strong, and wonderful.

Part 2 (19–37) applies that same focus on God's steadfast love and faithfulness to his dealings with the people of Israel, especially in his choice of David and his lineage. Just as the sun and the moon endure in the heavens, so David's throne shall endure on the earth (36–37). Nothing can destroy God's earthly purposes any more than it can bring the stars down from the heavens.

Part 3 (38–51), however, calls all of this into question or, rather, the psalmist calls God into question. "But now," begins the psalmist's lament (38): Now *everything I thought was true seems to be up for grabs. The kingdom is tottering. The throne is falling. The city is in ruins. Have you forgotten your promises? Have you forgotten* me?

Perhaps the entire purpose of the first thirty-seven verses—the enthusiastic rehearsal of God's steadfast love and faithfulness in the past—is to allow the psalmist to make his complaint about the present, much as a child can freely cry in pain so long as it is locked in its mother's firm embrace. Put another way, even while he is lamenting the upheaval and disorder of his current circumstances, the psalmist is nevertheless doing so under this banner of praise: *Misericordias Domini in aeternum cantabo.* The final verse (52), even if it belongs less to the psalm itself than to an editor's pen, concludes the whole of Book Three of the Psalter, making the final lines of Psalm 89 the declaration of an indisputable truth: "Blessed be the LORD for ever! Amen and Amen."

FROM THE FATHERS

Listen now how the prophet praises God at the very beginning of the psalm. He saw with his prophetic eyes the future iniquity of his people and the captivity that would be the consequence; yet he praised his own Lord for his unfailing promises. Through all this the prophet teaches that the promise was made by God on account of loving-kindness, and that the promise is faithful.

Theodoret of Cyr

As many signs as there are that trouble is near me;
As many failures as there are that haunt me;
As many sufferings as there are that cause me pain;
This I know, O God:

That there are countless more signs of your enduring love.

23

Monday of Advent IV
PSALM 65

Praise is due to thee,
O God, in Zion;
and to thee shall vows be performed,
O thou who hearest prayer!

vv. 1–2

PSALM 65 HAS BEEN CALLED A "SONG OF SPRINGTIME JOY" and it is easy to see why. You can almost picture the psalmist dancing with delight as spring rains bring the promise of an abundant harvest. All nature is smiling as the "river of God" (Ps. 65:9) flows through the land, softening the hardened soil of winter and infusing all that it touches with richness and hope (10). The poet can see in the rain from heaven the fruit it will yield in the fields of the earth. Each falling raindrop may as well be a full-grown grain of wheat. In the face of such blessing the psalmist is compelled to perform his vows in the temple, bring his thanksgiving, and sing praises to God (1).

To give thanks to the Lord was inseparable from giving him praise, which, in turn, was inseparable from giving God the whole of your life. Paying a "vow of thanksgiving" meant returning to

God a portion of those good things which God had given first. When God gives the harvest, the farmer gives back to God a portion of the yield. When God multiplies the flock, the shepherd gives back to God some of the sheep. When God blesses a life, the believer gives back to God the offering of his own heart.

To call thanksgiving a "vow," therefore, is to recognize that *giving* thanks is like making a gift of your life. Words are not enough. This is why the psalmist sees dwelling in the courts of the Lord as both the ultimate gift of God to man, as well as the ultimate gift of man to God (4). What richer blessing can be attained than to be welcomed into God's presence? What better response can be given in return than to accept that invitation and go into the house of God . . . with thanksgiving?

FROM THE FATHERS

"You crown the year with your bounty." Now in the Scriptures, the entire year is designated as the time of our salvation, in which we strive for an eternal reward. As the Savior says, he was sent in accordance with the words of Isaiah to preach the acceptable year of the Lord and the day of recompense. For in the present time . . . he will give the crown of everlasting blessing.

Bede

> *Your answers to my prayers, Lord,*
> *   are like so many raindrops that water the soil of my soul.*
> *Every need is like winter,*
> *But every answer is like spring.*
> *Eventually, the winter will pass,*

And the spring will endure,
    and your answers to my prayers will be like so many rivers,
      that will flood my soul with joy,
      and eventually run back to you!

24

Tuesday of Advent IV
PSALM 115

But we will bless the LORD from this time forth
and for evermore.

v. 18

T HE OPENING VERSE OF PSALM 115 SETS FORTH ITS
message: it is a song of praise in honor of the true God
who, unlike the nations' idols that are *made* by human
hands, is the only *Maker* of heaven and earth. Contained within
its verses are a satirical jab at false gods and those who trust in
them (2–8); a threefold confession of trust in the Lord (9–11);
a corresponding acclamation of blessing upon all the people of
God (12–14); an affirmation that God is the creator of all (15–16);
and a concluding declaration that God alone and forever will be
praised by the congregation of Israel (17–18).

This coherent structure is evidence of the psalm's liturgical
use. It is speculated that, as with many of the psalms, the verses
of the song were voiced by various groups and individuals in the
worshiping assembly. The opening verse is made by the entire
congregation: "Not to us, O LORD, not to us" (1). Then, someone
asks the question of verse 2: "Why should the nations say, 'Where

is their God?'" Another voice gives the answer (3–8), declaring that the true God is in heaven while the earth is populated only with false gods, idols made by human hands and imaginations. Three choirs, each in turn, call for trust in the Lord (9–11), after which the priest recites a blessing upon the people (12–15). It is left to the entire congregation to once again join in and finish the song, praising God for his work of creation and promising to praise him "from this time forth and for evermore!" (18).

Whatever the specific vocal choreography, it is clear that this is a psalm for the gathered community. Surrounded by nations who *put their trust in idols*, every time she prays, Israel confesses her faith in the Lord God who is one God (Deut. 6:4), who is the *helper and defender* of the house of Israel. All other "gods" play false with their devotees, for they can be no more reliable, strong, or wise than the people who make them. This is why idolatry is an abomination in the sight of God—not because the Lord is deprived of worship, but because his people are deprived of salvation. *Not to us, Lord, but to thy name give glory.*

FROM THE FATHERS

There is no falseness in God's promises because for the all-powerful there is no problem about doing things. And so the effects of the will are never lacking because the will itself is nothing other than power. Whatever God wills, he can do; he can do as much as he wishes.

Fulgentius of Ruspe

Father, I know that I put confidence in things that cannot help,
In places that cannot protect,
In people that cannot save.
There is only one true God—

   One true Helper, Protector, Savior.
Today, you and I will be about the business of cleaning house again.
All the idols eventually have to go,

   one more today,

   hopefully another one tomorrow.
Eventually . . . only you.

25

Wednesday of Advent IV
PSALM 81

O that my people would listen to me,
that Israel would walk in my ways!

v. 13

THE FIRST FIVE VERSES OF PSALM 81 ARE AN EXTENDED
call to worship. It is not clear for which Jewish festival.
What is clear is that it is to be a time of rejoicing and
remembrance. All the instruments of the temple are to be put to
use, including the shofar ("trumpet" in the RSV translation)—
those ubiquitous rams' horns used to signal the start of all festivals
and celebrations. The people's voices, too, of course—instruments
created by the hand of God—are to raise a song and shout for joy!

Once the psalmist has everyone's attention, however, his
words go in a dramatically different direction. In fact, they are
no longer the psalmist's words at all. From verse 6 to verse 16,
the unknown voice that speaks is God's. No other psalm contains
such a long message from the Almighty. You need to turn to the
prophets to find anything similar.

God reminds his listeners of that most pivotal and defining
event in their entire history—the exodus from Egypt. *I relieved you,*

he says. *I rescued you.* "I am the LORD your God, who brought you up out of the land of Egypt" (10). Though, at first, the psalmist was not familiar with the voice he heard—"I hear a voice I had not known" (5)—these words leave no question as to the identity of the Speaker.

In the midst of this brief recounting of the miracle of the Exodus, the Lord begins to make a point. *You called out to me in your distress, and I answered you* (7), *but, just like my people in the wilderness, you stopped listening to me. My people stopped listening to me in the desert, and you are not listening to me, either.*

The psalmist's audience would know exactly what the psalm is talking about. They knew the story well—of God's deliverance, of the people's rebellion, of their idolatry and unfaithfulness. Because they did not listen, they were given over to their enemies, and over to their own devices. They hungered and thirsted because their ears were deaf to the voice of their Deliverer. Perhaps, however, the psalm's listeners were not prepared for the indictment that they too are turning a deaf ear to their God.

"O that my people would listen to me" (13) is set in the present. This means, in *our* present as well. In Psalm 81, the call to *listen* is as strong, if not stronger, than the call to *praise.*

FROM THE FATHERS

"And he fed them with the fat of wheat." [God] led them into the land of promise. He fed them, not with manna as in the desert, but with the wheat that had fallen, and that had risen again. He is the wheat; he also is the rock who quenches the thirst of the Israelites in the desert. He satisfied their thirst spiritually with honey, and not with water, so that they who believe and receive the food taste honey in their mouth.

Jerome

Listening takes time, as you know, Lord,
and it takes real interest.
I feel a poverty of both.
The countless distractions are rampant.
The One attraction barely gets my attention.
That's my confession—but not the final word.
The final word is yours, Lord,
and that is what I will listen for.

26

Thursday of Advent IV
PSALM 93

The LORD reigns, he is robed in majesty;
the LORD is robed in majesty
and armed with strength.

v. 1 (NIV)

WHO THEN IS THIS, THAT EVEN WIND AND SEA OBEY him?" once asked the disciples (see Mk. 4:37–41). Mark tells us that, in the minutes just before, the suddenly storm-driven waves of the sea of Galilee were beating into their boat, beginning to fill it. A word of command from Jesus to the roiling waters—"Peace! Be still!"—calmed not only the waters but also the terrified hearts of the twelve. Who has such power and authority that with a simple command the roaring floods—both outside and inside—are silenced? The question is answered in Psalm 93.

"The Lord reigns," declares the psalmist. Another among the so-called "enthronement psalms," Psalm 93 celebrates the omnipotent rule of God—God is robed in majesty, girded with strength, and his authority is absolute. Notice how the voice of the psalm moves back and forth from speaking *about* God to speaking *to*

God, an indication of how it may have been used by solo and choir in the liturgy of the temple. One likely scenario is that the leader began, "The LORD reigns!" (1) to which a chorus of jubilant voices responded, "*Thy* throne is established from of old" (2). The leader calls out, "The LORD on high is mighty!" (4) to which the congregation adds the final word, "Holiness befits *thy* house, O LORD" (5).

In five succinct verses, a virtual cheer of praise is raised in the sanctuary. It could have gone on much longer, but rather than giving a lengthy list of the various aspects of creation over which the Almighty reigns, Psalm 93 lifts out a single image to make its point: the flood-swelled waters. In doing so, the psalmist takes his readers back to a "time" before time, when the earth was without form and void, when darkness was upon the face of the deep and the Spirit of God moved over the face of the waters (Gen. 1:1–2). More than any other force of nature, the primal flooding waters represent the world in chaos, before, by a simple word—"Let there be"—God brought order into being (see Gen. 1:6–8).

The author of Psalm 93 knew what roaring floods would mean to his readers. The sound of God's voice over the chaos, and the stories of God's control over some of the thunderous waters that came after—such as Noah and the flood, and Moses and the Red Sea—would immediately come to mind. Just as John knew, more than a thousand years later, when he wrote, "In the beginning was the Word" (John 1:1), that his readers would hear God speaking peace once again, this time robed in garments of flesh and girded with humility. However loud the floods may lift up their voice, there is a voice that is louder still. Who is this who speaks and all is silenced? How very similar the answers now seem: "The Lord reigns" and "Jesus is Lord."

FROM THE FATHERS

"Truly I say to you, henceforth you shall see the Son of man sitting at the right hand of the power of God." To sit at the right hand of the Father is a mystery belonging to the Incarnation. The seat on which the Lord Jesus was to sit was prepared from everlasting.

Rufinus of Aquileia

What new creation are you making of me, Lord?
What order are you bringing out of my chaos?
Speak, Lord, for—at least right now—
    your servant is listening.

27

Friday of Advent IV
PSALM 88

Thou hast put me in the depths of the Pit,
in the regions dark and deep.

v. 6

I N PSALM 88 WE APPROACH ONE OF THE DARKEST AND most desolate passages of the Psalter, and perhaps of the entire Bible. Unlike other psalms of lament in which the psalmist cries out for help, there is no resolution in these verses, no promise to trust in the Lord, no pledge to offer thanksgiving or to sacrifice an offering when deliverance comes. The psalm begins and ends on the bitter note of despair, and if you hope to find a tinge of relief somewhere in between, Psalm 88 is a disappointment. Image after image portrays a soul in torment, hopelessly alone and at the brink of death, forsaken by everyone, including God. The psalmist blames God for the circumstances that have brought on this diatribe and accusatively questions God's purposes behind it all. But no answers come.

In Psalm 88 God is silent, but the psalmist is not. This is still a prayer we are reading. It is not a complaint cast into the void, but rather one side of a conversation tenaciously brought before a seemingly unresponsive God. Three times the psalmist addresses God by name (1, 9, 13)—not about to let go of the Almighty until every ounce of emotion has been poured out. I am reminded of John Calvin's introduction to his commentary on the Psalms, where he writes:

> I have been accustomed to call this book, I think not inappropriately, "An Anatomy of all the Parts of the Soul"; for there is not an emotion of which any one can be conscious that is not here represented as in a mirror. Or rather, the Holy Spirit has here drawn to the light all the griefs, sorrows, fears, doubts, hopes, cares, perplexities, in short all the distracting emotions with which the minds of men are wont to be agitated. . . . The Psalms are replete with all the precepts which serve to frame our life to every part of holiness, piety, and righteousness, yet they will principally teach and train us *to bear the cross.*[2]

Speaking of the cross, I once heard Psalm 88 read by a friend to a group of us on pilgrimage in the Holy Land. The Church of St. Peter in Gallicantu (*cock's crow*) is built over the probable site of the house of Caiaphas, the High Priest. Just as countless thousands of pilgrims have done, we stood together underneath the house, in the bottom of a small but deep pit, thought possibly to have been the place where Jesus was imprisoned as he waited to be interrogated by his captors. Even now the scene comes back to me, and I recall my friend's sometimes trembling voice as he made his way through the psalm, line after painful line ringing off the stone walls that enclosed us. Our imaginations were afire. And then he came to the end. "You have taken from me friend and neighbor—darkness is my closest friend."[3] Without warning, the lights were turned out, and we stood together in the voiceless darkness.

FROM THE FATHERS
See how the verses of this psalm manifest the actual circumstances of Christ's passion.

Cyril of Jerusalem

> *You are sometimes silent, Lord.*
> *I think, today,*
> > *I will just take some time to be silent with you.*

28

Saturday of Advent IV
PSALM 63

Thou hast been my help,
and in the shadow of thy wings I sing for joy.

v. 7

THE SUPERSCRIPTION OF PSALM 63 SAYS IT IS A SONG of David, composed while he was "in the wilderness of Judah." There are two occasions in the histories of Samuel to which the psalm may apply: when David fled Saul, whose jealous rage was inciting him to murder (1 Sam. 23:14); and when David was under threat from his own son Absalom, who sought to wrest the throne for himself (2 Sam. 16:14). The psalm depicts its author wandering about the barren hills of Judah, recalling his former safe and intimate meetings with God in the tabernacle, in much the same way that a severely thirsty person might conjure up images of cold running water. The words are personal and filled with longing. The psalmist addresses himself directly to his God—"thou art *my* God"—and the reader is "let in" on the intimate exchange.

The metaphor of thirst (which appears in a number of psalms, e.g., 107, 143, and 42), though thoroughly human and understandable, may perhaps not carry the same sense of urgency in our own day. Within moments of reading this sentence, you can fill a glass with pure, cold water from the tap, and a second just as quickly. But for the ancient poet, the only hope of quenching his thirst depends on a fresh stream or a clean spring in the wilderness. And he might have to walk miles to find one.

The psalmist recalls the ease with which he once accessed God's presence by simply walking into the sanctuary (Ps. 63:2), much as we might walk to the sink and turn on the water faucet. But now, alone in the desert, he finds himself alienated from the tabernacle, separated from all of the surroundings that once brought him the sense of God's loving presence. What's more, even as he seeks the Lord, he is pursued by those he says "seek the hurt of my soul" (10, BCP).

Yet, even in his estrangement, the psalmist discovers that God is still his "helper," that God's wings, much like the wings of the cherubim in his beloved tabernacle, are still overshadowing him, even out here in the barren wilderness (7). The God of the sanctuary is also the God of the desert. Here, in the dry land, the psalmist will still lift up his hands in praise (4), he will still live to glorify God's name, he will still be satisfied with the fullness of God's loving-kindness (5).

FROM THE FATHERS

In the daytime, if we do remember [God], other cares and troubles entering in, drive the thought out again; but in the night it is possible to remember continually, when the soul is calm and at rest. . . . For it is indeed right to remember [God] throughout the day. But, inasmuch as you are always full of cares and distracted amid the things of this life, at least remember God on your bed; at the morning dawn, meditate on him.

John Chrysostom

You are the Bright and Morning Star, O Lord.
Your coming is like the dawn.
Though for these hours I sit in darkness,
I will greet you in the morning.

29

The Nativity of the Lord

PSALM 150

Let everything that breathes praise the LORD!
Praise the LORD!

v. 6

T HE PSALTER IS ACTUALLY A COLLECTION OF FIVE BOOKS of psalms, each of which ends with a brief doxology (see Ps. 41:13, 72:18–19, 89:52, 106:48). Considering all that has been said about the Lord God in the previous 149 psalms, what else can be said? Here, at the conclusion of the entire Psalter, what can possibly bear the weight of being the last word? Psalm 150—it is as if all of the previous doxologies have multiplied and expanded into one final and glorious eruption of jubilant praise.

The genius of this psalm is how much it says with so very few words. First, it answers all the basic questions about praising God: *where* God is to be praised—from this particular temple on earth to the highest of the heavens; *why* God is to be praised—for the excellence of his acts and for the excellence of his being; *how* God is to be praised—with every sound of music at our disposal; *who* is to praise God—all who breathe the breath of life.

Second, even as the psalmist is giving these succinct instructions, he is directing an ever-growing orchestra and chorus to perform the very things he is describing. This is a psalm not to be read but to be sung. This is not praise in theory (there is no such thing anyway); it is praise in practice! Can you hear the growing volume and the increasing sense of urgency as each new instrument is queued to add its voice to the symphony? The sound and tempo build with such momentum that, ironically, it feels as if you will be quite breathless by the time all who have breath are invited to join in.

Describing the sounds he heard in the courts of heaven, the writer of the book of Revelation again and again speaks of voices and calling and singing and crying aloud: "Then I heard what seemed to be the voice of a great multitude, like the sound of many waters and like the sound of mighty thunderpeals, crying, 'Hallelujah! For the Lord our God the Almighty reigns'" (Rev. 19:6). From time to time in the history of our salvation, heaven's doors are opened to earth, and the sound of angelic choruses slices through to the world's dull senses. The psalmists and prophets heard it. Some shepherds too. *Glory to God in the highest!*

If praise is the joyful recognition that *we* are not the center of the universe, the grateful acknowledgment that someone else is and always will be, then Psalm 150 is praise at its best. It is the best echo we can make on earth to the "new song" that is always being sung in heaven.

FROM THE FATHERS

The trumpet is the contemplative mind or the mind by which the teaching of the spirit is embraced. The harp is the busy mind that is quickened by the commands of Christ. The timbrel represents the death of fleshly desire because of honesty itself. Dancing is the agreement of reasonable spirits all saying the same thing and in which there are no divisions. . . . The melodious cymbal reflects the active mind affixed on its desire for Christ. The joyous cymbal is the purified mind inspired by the salvation of Christ.

Origen

O God,
Today I bring again the instruments of my heart and mind and body.
Teach them more of the song of all creation—
*   The song of angels, archangels, and all the company of heaven—*
Who forever sing in praise to you.
Then, tomorrow, teach them some more.

30

Feast of Saint Stephen

PSALM 31

Into thy hand I commit my spirit;
thou hast redeemed me, O LORD, faithful God.

v. 5

INTO THY HANDS I COMMIT MY SPIRIT" IS THE MOST well-known verse of this psalm. His own hands helplessly nailed to a cross, Jesus quoted it—with the all-important addition, "Father"—as he "breathed his last" upon the cross (Lk. 23:46). Stephen prayed much the same as he was being stoned to death, the first martyr of the fledgling church: "Lord Jesus, receive my spirit" (Acts 7:59). With these words of trusting relinquishment at its center, and read in the light of Jesus's passion and death— really, the consummation of his incarnation—the whole of Psalm 31 takes on a depth of meaning and significance that lends itself to our own use in especially difficult times of trouble or sorrow. If the Son of God himself found this prayer to be the perfect expression of his heart's desire for rest in the hands of his Father, could we find any more suitable expression for our own?

The psalmist uses images of God's hands to convey sanctuary from forces of destruction around him. To commit yourself into the hands of God is to entrust your whole life to God's *guidance*—"thy hand shall lead me, and thy right hand shall hold me" (139:10); God's *protection*—"thou dost stretch out thy hand against the wrath of my enemies, and thy right hand delivers me" (138:7); God's *mercy*—"let us fall into the hand of the LORD, for his mercy is great" (2 Sam. 24:14); and God's *blessing*—"in thy presence there is fulness of joy, in thy right hand are pleasures for evermore" (Ps. 16:11). The poet of Psalm 31 is clearly familiar with these and many other depictions of the "hand of the Lord."

With the change in tone in verses 10–20, the writer describes his depressing circumstances. He is literally being consumed by the sufferings that have come upon him, as his "bones waste away" (10). His weakness, his own iniquity, his enemies, even his neighbors, have all conspired to reject him, even to destroy him. Still, even in the midst of such dire straits, he confesses his trust in God by confidently declaring that his entire life and all of its circumstances are intimately known to and manageable by God, and not subject to the powers that would harm him: "My times are in *thy* hand; deliver me from the hand of my enemies" (15). This is the basis for the unwavering hope he displays in the closing verses of his song.

FROM THE FATHERS

God rescues and frees the one who puts his hope in him. He bends his ear to them, and he snatches them . . . so that they are saved.

Arnobius the Younger

Lord, there are "hands" that have hold of me
    that are too strong for me.
But my trust is in your promise:
    "For the LORD has ransomed Jacob,
        and redeemed him from hands too strong for him" (Jer. 31:11).
Your hand is the strongest of all,
And into your hand I commend my life,
       today . . . and always.

31

Feast of Saint John

PSALM 86

In the day of my trouble I call on thee,
for thou dost answer me.

v. 7

AT THE START OF PSALM 86, WE ARE INCLINED TO think we are reading an ordinary cry of lament. The psalmist is in some kind of trouble and turns to the Lord for assistance. But as we read further, we encounter a mixture of petition and praise that goes on through the entire psalm. The psalmist's situation may be dire, but good things have happened as well. *I am poor and needy; thou art good and forgiving* (1, 5). *I call on thee; thou dost answer me* (7). *Teach me thy way; thou, LORD, hast helped and comforted me* (11, 17). The psalm goes back and forth between calling out to God in need, and thanking God for needs that have already been met. One way to approach Psalm 86 is as the prayer of a fairly ordinary life, one with which we are all familiar.

There is no question the psalmist is in pain and urgently trying to get God's attention. The opening seven verses all sound like a soul urgently trying to get God's attention: incline your ear; preserve my life; you are my God; save your servant; be gracious;

gladden my soul; give ear, O Lord. But rather suddenly, with verse 8, the tone of voice is transformed, as if the psalmist begins to look at things from an entirely different perspective, namely God's: there is none like you; there are no works like yours; you art great and do wondrous things; you alone are God. Instead of asking for deliverance, now the psalmist gives praise: I give thanks to you; I will glorify your name. Even when the psalmist returns to his complaint in verse 14, the final four verses are a yin and yang of petition and praise, of *help me's* and *thank you's*.

Does this all sound somewhat familiar? Psalm 86 is less a formula for prayer than a description of a relationship—a relationship between God and God's servant. Most all of us can identify with the ups and downs in this psalm, and with the rapidity with which we make those descents and ascents. A *Help me, God* can be prayed in the same breath as a *Thank you, Lord* because each is part of a genuine relationship.

Verses 11 and 12 sit at the core of the psalm: "Unite my heart to fear thy name. I will give thanks to thee, O LORD my God, with my whole heart." Both our cries for help, and our thanksgiving for the help already rendered, are *united* in a heart that is wholly God's to begin with. In the end, the ease with which the psalmist moves back and forth between petition and praise is rooted in the stability of his relationship with God. The psalmist is as confident in God's love as he is dependent upon it. Need and trust—two ends of the same relationship of love.

FROM THE FATHERS

The only true divine healer of human sickness, the holy comforter of the soul when it is ill, is the Word of the Father. . . . Wisdom, the Word of the Father, who created human beings, concerns himself with the whole creation, and as the physician of the whole person heals both body and soul.

Clement of Alexandria

Sometimes, Lord, I feel like two different people,
  complaining one minute and thankful the next.
No surprise to you, I suppose,
  because you seem to listen to both.
So, unite my heart too, as the psalmist asked,
  so that, in whatever state I am,
  I will be wholly yours.

32

Feast of the Holy Innocents

PSALM 23

The LORD is my shepherd, I shall not want.

v. 1

THERE IS PROBABLY NO OTHER PSALM THAT HAS BEEN copied, recited in worship, prayed in private, and set to music more than Psalm 23. The tones of rest and trust that permeate its six short verses strike a resonant chord in every human heart, for they describe that world of contentment and serenity for which we all long. It is not a world that exists out there some*where*, however. It is a world that exists because of some*one*. It is the world created for his sheep by the Good Shepherd. The Lord is the maker of this world, and only because of his guiding hand and provision—his loving-kindness and mercy—do the sheep dwell within its blessed gates.

The self-sacrificial love of the good shepherd for his sheep and his limitless dedication to their well-being was common knowledge in the ancient Middle East. The psalmist turns to this familiar pastoral image to describe the depth of attention God gives to those under his care— even the weakest and the smallest. This is not the image of a hired servant who considers himself of more value than his flock. This is the image of the good shepherd who knows each sheep by name and who does not hesitate to *lay down his life* for any one of them (John 10:12–15).

The psalmist takes an interesting turn of language in the middle of his song. For the first three verses, it is as if the poet is telling those nearby about the all-sufficient care of the Lord: he provides for me; he leads me; he restores my soul; he brings me forth. This is the testimony of someone fed in the lush pastures of God's grace and refreshed with the cool waters of his mercy: *You who will listen, let me tell you*—the Lord *is my shepherd.*

Then, in the face of the darkest trial of all—the overshadowing presence of death—it is as if the poet turns from those listening and looks into the face of the Shepherd: *Because you are with me, I am not afraid. Even here, in this valley of loss, I lack nothing, for you are with me. And when at last my life here does run out, I will still be full, for I will be in your house. Lord, you are my Shepherd.*

FROM THE FATHERS
When you say, "The Lord is my shepherd," no proper grounds are left for you to trust in yourself.

Augustine

> *"The good shepherd lays down his life for the sheep."*
> *These are your words, Lord.*
> *Is it too much to think that you had me in mind when you spoke them?*
> *Hardly holy, and certainly not innocent,*
>   *but still your child . . . your lamb.*

You had me in mind,
    and for that I will forever be grateful.
Really . . . forever.
    You are my Shepherd.
    How full can one's life possibly be?

33

December 29

PSALM 19

Let the words of my mouth and the meditation of my heart
be acceptable in thy sight.

v. 14

HOW ARE YOU TO KNOW AND BRING YOUR LIFE into harmony with the ways of God? In some of the most poetically descriptive language of the psalmody, Psalm 19 unfolds a three-part answer to this question. The varying structures and vocabularies of the psalm reveal distinct styles that have been merged to create a single voice of prayer, an eloquent triptych that moves the reader from a general acknowledgment of God's ways to a personal commitment to live by them.

In part one, verses 1–6, the psalmist describes the splendor of the heavens as a vehicle for displaying the glory of God. Interestingly, in these verses, the psalmist speaks of God only once, using the generic name, *El.* The emphasis is on the created order—its silence more articulate than any sound. The joyful rhythm of the rising and setting sun represents the knowledge of God's presence and oversight through all creation, including the lives of men and women. God reveals his ways in the marvels of his handiwork, and nothing escapes his notice. Psalm 19 portrays creation as a divine masterpiece that reveals the character of its maker. If you want to learn the ways of God, the heavens are a good place to start.

Part two, verses 7–10, leads the reader into a more personal encounter with God. The name of God, repeated six times, is now *Yahweh*, the name by which he revealed himself to the Jewish people, not only as creator but as deliverer. More precisely, *Yahweh* established a covenant with this nation, a relationship of love and commitment that is rooted in the Lord's revealed word. In a flowing cadence of phrases, the psalmist speaks of God's law, testimony, precepts, commandments, and ordinances, all different terms for the *Torah*, God's own word revealed to God's own people. This word, says the psalmist, is perfect, sure, right, pure, clean, and true. No wonder it is desirable, for God's ways are found in its sounds.

In part three, verses 11–14, the psalm turns intensely personal. Under the scrutiny of the sun's daily heat and in the light of God's ever-present word, who can stand by as an innocent observer, untouched—unburned even—by their convicting light? When God's light shines on me, the distance between his ways and my ways comes into sharp focus, says the psalmist. I must ask for help to close the gap. With this prayer on his lips, the psalmist ends his song by addressing God as "redeemer," *gō'ēl*, a technical term for a next of kin who is responsible to buy back his relative from slavery (Lev. 25:48–49) and to avenge the murder of a kinsman (Num. 35:16–28). By the end of the psalm, God is addressed neither as a distant creator, nor even as the Lord of a nation, but as a member of the family.

By taking us on a journey from the infinite expanse of the heavens to the deepest recesses of the human heart, the psalmist draws an artistic map for following God, and for bringing our lives into harmony with God's ways. It is no wonder that C. S. Lewis considered Psalm 19 to be "the greatest poem in the Psalter and one of the greatest lyrics in the world."[4]

FROM THE FATHERS

If you observe a most mighty and magnificent building, you admire the builder; and if you see a skillfully and beautifully designed ship, you think of the shipwright; and at the sight of a painting the painter comes to mind. Much more, to be sure, does the sight of creation lead the viewers to the Creator.

Theodoret of Cyr

Lord, it seems that getting to know you can be
　　a dangerous business.
Still, I'm not sure there is anything
　　I want more.
What I say . . . what I do . . . who I am,
　　redeem them all.
Buy them all back,
　　for yourself.

34

December 30

PSALM 113

He raises the poor from the dust,
and lifts the needy from the ash heap.

v. 7

PSALM 113 PRESENTS US WITH THE JUXTAPOSITION of two seemingly contrasting wonders about the nature of God—his incomparable majesty and his tender mercy. To describe them, the psalmist draws upon a very familiar social concept: status. The Lord rules in glory from on high, yet lives among the poorest of the poor.

The psalm opens with a call to praise the Lord, perhaps directed by one of the temple priests to the choir of cantors (1). Their response builds rapidly into a crescendo of sound, glorifying God for his rule over all time and space (2–4). Their repeated use of "the *name* of the LORD" shows the profound deference they are paying to the One who is so inconceivably superior to them that they dare not even pronounce his name. But, the majesty of the Almighty is not the only, or perhaps even the chief, reason for praising him.

Verse 5 introduces the second half of the psalm with a rhetorical question: *Yes, God sits above even the heavens, making him unique in all the universe and beyond. But even more impressive, who else can sit so very high in glory and then stoop so very low in humility?* We praise the God who is beyond all time and space, but nevertheless makes his home in the lowest places of the earth—the hearts of the simple, the poor, the lost, the forsaken. God delivers his mercy eye-to-eye with the lowly and, once at that subordinate level, he turns the world upside down. The simple are made to be princes, the poor are seated with royalty, the barren become fruitful, and children lead the way into heaven. No wonder Mary sang, in anticipation of the incarnate Son of God, "he has put down the mighty from their thrones, and exalted those of low degree" (Lk. 1:52).

FROM THE FATHERS

To [the wise person], God, who knows the time of the harvest, is always good. Therefore, like a good farmer, he plows his fields by his abstinence; he clears his land by cutting off all vices; and he manures the field by humbling himself to the earth, for he knows that "God raises the needy from the earth and lifts up the poor out of the dunghill." . . . And so, to him, God is always good because he always hopes for good things from God.

Ambrose

You know that I sometimes lose sight of your goodness, Lord.
Nothing has changed about you, of course.
But my eyes get clouded by my weeping,
And my mind gets darkened by my thinking.

From morning to evening, though, you are the same.

   —the same in love, in mercy, in power . . . in goodness.

So I bless your name, Lord,

   From this time to the next,

   And every time after that.

35

*December 3*1
PSALM 90

So teach us to number our days
that we may get a heart of wisdom.

v. 12

T HERE ARE FIVE "BOOKS" IN THE COLLECTION THAT IS
the Psalter, and Psalm 90 is the first psalm of Book IV.
Both Jewish and Christian scholarship notes that the
emphasis of the final two books (sixty-one psalms in all) is on
God's sovereignty and glory. Three begin with the words *The* LORD
reigns (93, 97, 99), and the only ten psalms beginning with *Praise*
the LORD are in these closing volumes. Psalm 90 was chosen as a
fitting introduction to these songs of praise, and its title tells us
why: "God's Eternity and Human Frailty."

For creatures of dust we are remarkably blind to matters of our
own mortality. We spend a good part of our young lives oblivious
to death, unconsciously savoring the naive notion that life is meant
to be forever. Then, in the middle of our lives, circumstances
cause us to begrudgingly acknowledge death's presence. Perhaps,
understandably, we keep it standing outside the door, our backs
turned to it like some unwelcome visitor. Usually (and perhaps

fortunately) it is not until the arrival of old age and the frailties it brings with it, that we turn and come face to face with the reality that the spans of our lives are limited—that our days are "numbered" and, actually, quite few.

The superscription of Psalm 90 says: "A prayer of Moses, the man of God." If, in fact, Moses is the author of this psalm (other songs of Moses may be found in Exodus 15 and Deuteronomy 32), then we are hearing the voice of a man who has lived long past the fourscore years that even the strongest might expect (Ps. 90:10). In any case, we have the prayer of a man who stands at the end of his days. From that vantage point, looking both forward and backward to the horizons of his life, he sees with a profound clarity two unalterable truths: that the life of a person—*his* life—will pass away like the dying grass or like a night's dream; and that God alone is everlasting. In contrast to the incessant change and decay that defines human mortality—and which the psalmist knows firsthand—only God and his "glorious majesty" (17, BCP) remain changeless and eternal. Knowing these truths—numbering our own days and living for the Ancient of Days (Dan. 7:9)—this, says the psalmist, is the substance of wisdom (12).

FROM THE FATHERS

Whatever there is in the world, it fades away, it passes. As for this life, what is it but what the psalmist said: "In the morning it will flower, but in the evening it will fall." That is what "all flesh is" [Isa. 40:6]. That is why Christ; that is why new life; that is why eternal hope; that is why the consolation of immortality has been promised us.

Augustine

> *O God, teach me the wisdom that comes from knowing*
>   *my own limits . . . and your own limitlessness.*
> *For you confined yourself within my house of clay*
>   *so that I might be set free within your house of light.*
> *The first house crumbles to dust.*
> *The last house will shine forever.*
> *Teach me the wisdom that comes from knowing both.*

36

January 1
PSALM 147

It is good to sing praises to our God;
for he is gracious, and a song of praise is seemly.

v. 1

WHEN THE PEOPLE OF ISRAEL DREW NEAR TO THE END of their journey in the wilderness, Moses prepared them for what lay ahead by reminding them of what had brought them to this point. After generations of slavery in Egypt, they were now a free people, great in number and filled with promise. They carried with them the wealth of their oppressors and stood on the verge of possessing the land promised to their fathers. Lest they succumb to thinking that their own hand had accomplished their deliverance, Moses reminded them of the true reason for their good fortune: "It was not because you were more in number than any other people that the LORD set his love upon you and chose you, for you were the fewest of all peoples; *but it is because the LORD loves you*, and is keeping the oath which he swore to your fathers" (Deut. 7:7–8).

One can hear the echo of Moses's words in the verses of Psalm 147. The second of the final five psalms of the Psalter—called the Praise Psalms because each begins and ends with the same jubilant shout, "Praise the LORD!" (*Hallelujah!*)—Psalm 147 reminds the people both of their humble roots and of their great destiny. A people who have been made by God's hand, healed by God's mercy, and preserved by God's power have nothing to boast of in themselves. Praising God is one of the surest correctives to human pride. With both hands lifted to God, there isn't one left to pat yourself on the back.

The psalmist summons praise for the God whose power is most gloriously revealed in his love. He calls each lofty star by its own name (4); he attends to each downtrodden soul. The outcasts, the brokenhearted, the wounded, all find their appointed place within God's gathered house (2–6). Creation's highest and lowest are assured of the Lord's care. It is not worthiness but weakness that brings down the love of God from the heavens. And this is an enduring truth for which God's praises should always be sung because God and people look at power differently. The psalmist recognizes that it is tempting to place your security in physical might and human strength (10), and these are of no importance from God's point of view. The strongest force in all the universe is the mercy of God, and those who place their trust in that power will always be giving thanks.

FROM THE FATHERS

"Who heals the contrite of heart, who binds up their wounds." A wonderful mode of healing is announced, so that if we wish to be restored we must make ourselves contrite in a most vigorous way. This contrition, however, is aimed at renewal and leads to full recovery; what transcends every blessing, it admits the Physician who grants eternal health. . . . The heavenly Physician treats the hearts of penitents when they are battered with heavy affliction. He binds and strengthens them by wrapping them with the bandage of his devoted love, and impels them to the strongest hope of recovery.

Cassiodorus

Lord, you know the wounds in my heart,
(Most of them self-inflicted),
All of them from that fall.
But here I am, standing up and walking again.
　　So a song of praise seems like just the right thing.

37

January 2
PSALM 46

"Be still, and know that I am God."

v. 10

SOMETIME AROUND 1529 THE CHURCH REFORMER and former Augustinian monk Martin Luther paraphrased Psalm 46 into one of the most beloved hymns of Protestantism: *Ein' feste Burg ist unser Gott.* Later translated into English, the opening words are:

A mighty fortress is our God,
   A bulwark never failing;
Our helper he, amid the flood
   Of mortal ills prevailing.[5]

Psalm 46 is one of liturgical psalms in praise of Mount Zion, God's "dwelling place" (see also Psalms 48, 76, 84, 87, and 122). The common theme running through these psalms is the incomparable beauty and unshakable security of the City of God. The place where God makes his abode is the most glorious and the most stable place in all the universe. To live within its borders is to live without fear, for nothing in all creation—not the volatile power of nature or that of man, or (in Luther's words) the destructive power of "our ancient foe"—can do harm to those who dwell in "the holy habitation of the Most High" (Ps. 46:4).

Human security, affirms the poet, can be grounded in the sovereign omnipotence of God. Where God is, there is no reason to fear. And, since God is "with us" (7), we need fear no place. In just a few short verses, the psalmist effectively pulls the sharp teeth from all human anxiety. What threat can subdue the faith of those whose "hope and strength" is God?

And who is this God in whom the psalmist tells us to put our trust? The refrains of verses 7 and 11 tell us it is the "LORD of hosts"—the creator and ruler of all principalities and powers in the heavenly places (Col. 1:16). This is the "God of Jacob" (Ps. 46:7, 11)—the God of the patriarchs and prophets, the maker of the covenant, the deliverer of Israel, and the Lord of history. *All* authority in heaven and on earth belongs to God alone. So, to all the unruly forces at work in the world, he commands, *"Be still"* (the Hebrew literally means to desist, to surrender), and know this for certain: *"I am God"* (10).

We who sing either the psalm or the hymn do well to remember that these are songs in praise of not a strong faith but a strong God. Human trust and confidence, like mountains and seas, can be shaken, and often are. But the God in whom we place even our weakest hope, our most trembling reliance, is immovable and always "very present" (1).

FROM THE FATHERS

There are many kinds of tribulation, and in all of them we must seek refuge in God, whether the trouble concerns our income, our bodily health, some danger threatening those we love or something we need to support our life. Whatever it is, there should be no refuge for a Christian other than our Savior. He is God, and when we flee to him, we are strong. No Christian will be strong in himself or herself; but God, who has become our refuge, will supply the strength.

Augustine

All my hope is in you alone, O Lord.
And, where I have put it in anything or anyone less than you,
    help me take it back,
       and put it where it belongs.

38

January 3
PSALM 91

My refuge and my fortress;
my God, in whom I trust.

v. 2

D RAWING UPON AN ALREADY FAMILIAR PATTERN
in the sixth century, St. Benedict directed in his rule
for monastery life that Psalm 91 be sung at the hour
of Compline, the night service of prayer that closed every day of
the week. Here, most certainly, is a prayer that "puts the church to
bed," with confident assurance in the all-encompassing protection
of God. It is, above all, a song of trust. If there is a New Testament
counterpart to its succinct message, it would be found in Paul's
rhetorical questions to the Romans: "If God is for us, who is
against us? . . . Who shall separate us from the love of Christ?"
(Rom. 8:31, 35). The self-evident answer for both Paul and the
psalmist is: *nothing.*

In Psalm 91, we sometimes hear the voice of the psalmist
confessing his faith in God: "For thou, LORD, art my hope" (9,
BCP). Sometimes we hear the voice of another, as if reminding the
psalmist of God's loving oversight: "For he shall give his angels

charge over thee" (11, BCP). And sometimes, as at the end of the psalm, we hear the voice of God himself telling anyone who will listen that he has made a promise to his servant: "I will protect him . . . I will answer him; I will be with him . . . I will rescue him" (14–15).

Someone has suggested that the vocabulary of protection was virtually plundered for the composition of this poem—*stronghold, deliverance, defend, faithfulness, shield, hope, charge over, bear thee, salvation.* These describe the sovereign love of a God who, again and again, has intervened unfailingly on behalf of his endangered beloved. Images arise of Noah's ark shut securely against the seething floodwaters; the ramparts of the divided Red Sea plunging down upon Pharaoh's horsemen; the cloudy and fiery pillars guiding the children of Israel through the desert; the walls of Jericho crumbling at the sound of Joshua's ram's horns; the true-flying stone of a shepherd boy striking silent the blasphemous voice of Goliath. Israel's whole history is contained within this psalm, as is the history of all those who have been grafted by grace into her sheltered vine (see Rom. 11:17). "For I am sure that neither death, nor life, nor angels, nor principalities, nor things present, nor things to come, nor powers, nor height, nor depth, nor anything else in all creation, will be able to separate us from the love of God in Christ Jesus our Lord" (Rom. 8:38–39).

FROM THE FATHERS

For if I am made just, no one can frighten me; I am afraid of nothing else, if I fear God. For "I shall not be afraid of the nocturnal fear, nor the dart which flies during the day, nor the terror which walks in the darkness nor the ruin and the midday demon." . . . You see the steadfastness and vigor of the soul that keeps the commandments of God and has confidence in the freedom that God gives.

Origen

You are my refuge, Lord, my only safety and shelter.
I know that if I dwell with you—in you—
Any and every affliction that comes can be made into salvation

39

January 4
PSALM 87

Glorious things are spoken of you,
O city of God.

v. 3

VERY YEAR, WHEN WE CELEBRATE THE FEAST OF THE
dedication of our monastery church, the Church of the
Transfiguration, we read these words from Paul's letter to
the Ephesians: "So then you are no longer strangers and sojourners,
but you are fellow citizens with the saints and members of the
household of God, built upon the foundation of the apostles and
prophets, Christ Jesus himself being the cornerstone" (Eph. 2:19–
20). The imagery of a physical building as the house of God is part
of what has made this passage fitting for the dedication of a church
for almost two millennia. But if we limit ourselves to envisioning
only the beauty of stone walls and the strength of wooden beams
we miss the larger point. Paul is writing about the miraculous
inclusion of the Gentiles, of *all* peoples, into the family that God
birthed through Abraham and Sarah. Those whose ancestry hadn't
a single drop of Jewish blood found themselves inheriting the
family fortune. Put another way, building materials that belonged

on the scrap pile were salvaged, retrofitted, and securely fastened to the structure of God's temple on earth. Things that had no business in the house of God were turned into showpieces.

The apostle Paul was not the first to describe the largess of God's heart in this way. Consider Psalm 87, a song in praise of Jerusalem, the divinely chosen city of God. Upon this mountain, God's favor rests. It is like no other place on earth. God founded a city for his own people, a dwelling place for the family who called him Father. Here, the lineage of Abraham made their home.

But, according to the psalmist's vision, as we enter the city's sacred gates, what do we find? These inhabitants don't look alike at all. They seem to come from everywhere: north, south, east, west. Even more surprising, we see walking side by side with Jacob's children some of their mortal enemies—Egyptians (Rahab, see Isa. 30:7), Babylonians, and even Philistines. We might be able to stretch our imaginations enough to see these "strangers and sojourners" as refugees, for a time finding asylum in the city of peace. But as they all move to the city center, we see a figure sitting with a large book in his lap, checking off every name—even the foreign names—as he emphatically declares, *Yes, he was* born *here,* and, *Yes, this is the city of her* birth. God himself is registering each of these people not only as citizens but as sons and daughters. And as he does so, their walking turns to dancing and they begin to sing: *The Jerusalem above is free, and she is our mother!* (see Gal. 4:26). *All of our springs are in her.*

FROM THE FATHERS

Since the psalmist said, "Glorious things are spoken of you, O city of God," and we understand this city to be the church, gathered together from all the nations, the psalm now speaks of the calling of the Gentiles. "I will be mindful of Rahab and Babylon among those that know me." Let the sinner be at peace, for the Lord was mindful of Rahab.

Jerome

Father, my name is in your book.
It got there because you wrote it there,
> *even before I was born.*
And there, next to it, you have written the place of my birth—
"The heart of God," it says.
All who are born here,
> *have a home forever.*

40

January 5
PSALM 100

Shout for joy to the LORD, all the earth.
Worship the LORD with gladness.
vv. 1–2 (NIV)

P SALM 100 IS THE FINAL IN A SERIES OF PSALMS (95–100)
that have been grouped together to celebrate the glorious
reign of God over all heaven and earth. Remember that the
Psalter is actually a prayer book that editors carefully arranged in
order to make it most useful for worship in the temple. (Other
groupings like this include Psalms 113–118, 120–134, and 146–
150.) In some ways, the whole of Psalm 100 has already appeared
in the psalms that precede it: make a joyful noise (Ps. 98:4); be
glad in the Lord (96:11–12); the invitation to come into God's
presence (95:6; 96:8); we are God's sheep and are pastured under
his care (95:7); give thanks to the Lord (95:2; 97:12); bless God's
name (96:2); God's mercy endures forever (98:3). It is as if Psalm
100 takes all of the major sounds already present in the previous
songs and, in only a few lines, piles them on top of one another
into a single and brilliant chord of praise to God.

Almost for certain, Psalm 100 was meant to be sung as the assembly of worshipers approached the temple in a grand procession of movement, voices, colors (all the priests in their flowing vestments) and sounds (the instruments all present as well). A liturgical cacophony! The occasion is as festive as it gets. What is the ruckus all about? The people of God are confessing their faith, declaring the truths upon which their entire lives are built: the Lord is God; the Lord made us and we belong to him; the Lord is always good, his mercy and faithfulness never come to an end. These provide reason enough for the people of God to rejoice in song. Still, there are not enough voices. Such an occasion demands everyone's attendance—make a joyful noise, *all* the earth.

I remember chanting this psalm as a child, as part of my tradition's Sunday morning prayer. I remember because of an odd turn of phrase in the psalm that always struck me as self-evident: "Be ye sure that the LORD he is God; it is he that hath made us, and not we ourselves." (3, BCP[6]) "Of course I'll be sure that God is God," I would think to myself. "Who else possibly could be?" And as for making myself? "Well, that is just ridiculous. Who in their right mind would think such a thing?" Decades have gone by since then, and the usual amount of childlike innocence has gone with them. Now, whenever I come to this verse of the psalm, whatever translation I may be reading, that earlier version comes to mind, and with it, a knowing smile almost always comes to my lips. I get it now.

FROM THE FATHERS

I spoke to all the things that are above me, all that can be admitted by the door of the senses, and I asked, "Since you are not my God, tell me about him. Tell me something of my God." Clear and loud they answered, "God is he who made us." I asked these questions simply by gazing at these things, and their beauty was all the answer they gave.

Augustine

Lord, today I want my voice to be added to this chorus of praise.
There are some things in my life that could silence me—you know them.
And there are some things in my heart, too, that could keep me mute.
But I don't want any of them, inside or out, to shut me down,
    or shut me up.
You are God.
You made me.
Your love endures . . . I want my praise to endure as well.

41

The Epiphany of the Lord
PSALM 72

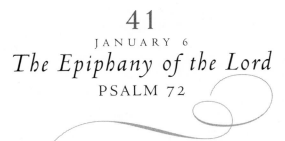

May all kings fall down before him,
all nations serve him!

v. 11

P SALM 72 IS THE CULMINATION OF BOOK II IN THE Psalter, which began with Psalm 42, called the "prayers of David" (20)—not that David necessarily wrote all these psalms, but they at least represent the spirit of David's hopes and desires before the Lord. They are in keeping with a heart that followed after God's own heart (see 1 Sam. 13:14; 16:7). Scholars tell us that Psalm 72 probably was written for the coronation of a king of Judea and Israel, perhaps even by David himself for his son Solomon. In any case, the prayer came to be used at the coronation ceremonies of subsequent kings, and possibly at the yearly anniversaries as well.

This is a prayer for God's blessing to rest upon his chosen royal agent. In the psalmist's world, the king was considered God's own appointed representative, bringing heavenly rule to earth and making God's heavenly purposes come to pass on earth. His rule was to bring justice to the people, fruitfulness to the land, and peace to all the nations. God's chosen monarch was to vanquish all enemies, raise up all the downtrodden, and free all the oppressed. All other kings would bring him gifts and bow down before him.

When the archangel Gabriel addressed the Virgin Mary, he announced that the child she would bear was to fulfill all of these prayers. "He will be great," the angel declared, "and will be called the Son of the Most High; and the Lord God will give to him the throne of his father David, and he will reign over the house of Jacob forever; and of his kingdom there will be no end" (Lk. 1:32–33). There is no question that the kind of reign envisioned by Psalm 72 is far beyond mortal means. Doesn't the psalm describe a kingdom that can only be achieved by one who is anointed by God, chosen by God, who in fact *is* God? For this reason, Psalm 72 is a regular feature in the liturgies of Christmas and Epiphany (as are Psalms 2 and 110), for it describes poetically the eternal reign of the Messiah over all the nations. Today, even as we conclude the Advent and Christmas seasons, we remember the bigger picture of God's saving work. The shadows of winter can be cast only within the radiance of God's Epiphany on earth. How fitting, then, is the benediction of verses 18 and 19, the concluding lines both of Book II of the psalms, and of these reflections—*Blessed be the glorious name of the Lord forever; may his glory fill the whole earth! Amen and Amen!*

FROM THE FATHERS

We are taught, therefore, to be of good cheer when we are afflicted in the world. We learn that the reason for being of good cheer is this: the world has been conquered and, of course, is subject to him who conquered it. For this reason, all the nations, set free from those who formerly controlled them, serve him, because "he delivered the poor from the mighty" through his own passion, "and the needy who had not helper."

Origen

Today I join the psalmist in blessing your name, O Lord.
    for your power and for your mercy;
    for your justice and for your compassion;
    for your rule and for your service.
All I know of prosperity, of peace, and of blessing,
    is because of you.
Why would I wish or allow any other to reign in my heart?

Who Are the Church Fathers Quoted in This Book?

AMBROSE (ca. 339–Good Friday, 397), Bishop of Milan

As the son of a Praetorian prefect in Gaul (modern France), Ambrose embarked on a civil career that eventually took him to Milan, where he served as governor of that region. When the bishop died, Ambrose was pressed by the Milanese people to become the new bishop, even though at the time he was only a *professed* Christian, not yet baptized or ordained. He is considered one of the original four doctors of the Western Church (together with Augustine, Jerome, and Gregory the Great), and for his contribution to the early growth of Christian hymns, he has been called "the Father of Liturgical Hymnody."

ARNOBIUS THE YOUNGER (d. after 451)

Little is known of Arnobius, usually referred to as "the Younger" and sometimes called "Junior," to distinguish him from the fourth-century Christian theologian of the same name. He was a monk who probably fled from the Vandals invading his native Africa and, from about 432, spent his remaining years in Rome. Some of his writings reveal his opposition to Augustine's doctrine of predestination, though he may be best known for his commentary on the Psalms which, in keeping with the practice of his time, is filled with allegorical and mystical interpretations.

ATHANASIUS (ca. 295–373), Bishop of Alexandria

Athanasius, who was born and raised in Alexandria and served there as a deacon, was made bishop by the popular acclaim of the city's Christians. Despite such initial support, the theological and political controversies of his time forced Athanasius into exile a total of five times. This probably worked to the overall benefit of the church, however, for it was during his years away that Athanasius did the bulk of his writing. He is considered one of the four doctors of the Eastern Church (together with the three hierarchs: Basil the Great, Gregory of Nazianzus, and John Chrysostom).

AUGUSTINE (354–430), Bishop of Hippo

One of the most distinguished and influential theologians of the Christian church, Augustine came to faith only after first rejecting the Christian influence of his mother and spending his early years philosophically and morally wandering. Still, he was a seeker, and after a renewed reading of the Scriptures (especially the letters of Paul) and the *Life of St. Antony* (written by Athanasius), and hearing the sermons of Ambrose, Augustine was baptized on Easter in 387. After spending some time as a monk (he would later write a rule for community life), he was ordained a priest, and later made bishop of Hippo in 395.

BEDE (ca. 673–735)

Considered to be the most influential scholar of Anglo-Saxon England, Bede, known as "the Venerable," began his studies at the age of seven, when he was given as an "oblate" to the newly founded monastery of Wearmouth. There, and subsequently at the monastery of Jarrow, he was given a broad classical education, and was eventually ordained a deacon at age nineteen and a priest at age thirty. Perhaps best known as the author of *An Ecclesiastical History of the English People*, the principal source for the study of the early English church, Bede was also a prominent Scripture scholar and teacher, as evidenced by his numerous writings, including works on the Psalms.

CASSIODORUS (ca. 485–ca. 580),
Roman statesman and church scholar

Flavius Magnus Aurelius Cassiodorus was a Roman statesman in one of the most turbulent periods of the Christian West. His life may be divided into two distinct periods: his early political years, when in various capacities he served the Ostrogothic kings in Italy; and his later scholarly monastic years, when he served the church, founded a monastery, and promoted the monastic disciplines of study and manuscript copying. His monumental *Expositio Psalmorum* (which took him more than ten years to write) is a complete commentary on the Psalms.

CYRIL (ca. 315–386), Bishop of Jerusalem

Cyril was raised in a Christian home, probably in Caesarea of Palestine, and rose through the ranks of the clergy, eventually being named a bishop sometime after 350. Despite three periods of banishment due to the theological controversies of his time, Cyril returned each time to his see in Jerusalem, where he eventually died. The most important surviving works of Cyril are a series of instructions given to candidates for Baptism during Lent and on

Holy Saturday, and a set of teachings given to the newly baptized during the week after Easter. Even today, these catechetical instructions are used to help prepare for and understand the Sacrament of Baptism.

EUSEBIUS OF CAESAREA (ca. 260–ca. 339),
Bishop of Caesarea and church historian

A controversial figure in the theological disputes of his time, Eusebius is nevertheless celebrated in both the East and West as the "Father of Church History." He is the author of many writings, the best known of which is his *Ecclesiastical History* in which he traces (through ten volumes!) the history of Christianity from the time of the apostles down to his own day. Though history was his favored topic, Eusebius also wrote on biblical topics, including a series of commentaries on the Psalms.

FULGENTIUS (ca. 467–533), Bishop of Ruspe

Born into a family of Roman senatorial rank, Fulgentius seemed destined to a life of civil service. But at the age of twenty-two, after reading a sermon by Augustine on Psalm 36, on the transitory nature of this earthly life, Fulgentius left his home and family to become a monk. His reputation as a spiritual guide and as a wise administrator drew the attention of others and, in 507, he was made Bishop of Ruspe (in North Africa). In addition to his pastoral duties, he devoted time to study and writing, drawing especially on Augustine, Ambrose, and Leo the Great to contribute his own treatises defending theological orthodoxy, promoting asceticism, and discussing spiritual principles.

GREGORY OF NAZIANZUS (ca. 329–390)

Basil the Great, his younger brother Gregory (of Nyssa), and this Gregory make up the three great fourth-century leaders of Christian orthodoxy known as the Cappadocian Fathers. (Cappadocia is now central Turkey.) Following a rich and varied education, that included time in Athens where he befriended Basil, Gregory would spend most of his adult life moving back and forth between the quiet, ascetic life of a monk, and the public ministry of a priest and bishop. In the end, his monastic vocation prevailed as he finished his final years in retreat at his home in Nazianzus, but not before his work as a preacher and writer had left its mark on the church.

JEROME (ca. 345–420), biblical scholar

Born Eusebius Hieronymus, Jerome's early Christian life was spent living the ascetic life with a group of friends in the Roman city of Aquileia. From there he set out for Palestine in 374, but settled for a time as a hermit in the Syrian desert (where he learned Hebrew so that he could better study the Scriptures). He was ordained a priest, worked for a time in Constantinople and in Rome, and finally settled in Bethlehem where he founded a monastery for men, living by himself in a cave near the traditional birthplace of Jesus. While known especially for his Latin translation of the Bible (the Vulgate), Jerome is also the author of numerous commentaries on the Scriptures, including notes and homilies on the Psalms.

JOHN CHRYSOSTOM (ca. 347–407),
Bishop of Constantinople

John was born in Antioch and, until he was made bishop of Constantinople in 398, he spent his entire life and ministry in and around this important city. He was baptized at eighteen and, after some years learning and living the life of an ascetic, which included time as a hermit in the mountains outside the city, he was ordained and appointed the preacher for the cathedral. His skill and dedication to this vocation earned him the name Chrysostom ("golden mouth"). From those and subsequent years, we have a large collection of his homilies on the various festivals of the church, the Gospels, the Acts of the Apostles, Paul's letters, and the Psalms.

ORIGEN (ca. 185–ca. 251)

Origen was one of the most learned teachers and perhaps the most prolific writer of the early church. He was born of Christian parents in Alexandria where his father was killed during the persecution of 202. Origen himself was prevented from surrendering to martyrdom only by his mother's intervention when she hid his clothes. He embraced a life of asceticism, sometimes severe, along with an intense career of teaching, preaching, and writing, which culminated in the establishment of a school in Caesarea in 231. He died during the persecution of the emperor Decius in 250, after suffering prolonged imprisonment and torture. Among Origen's many writings were commentaries on almost every book of the Bible, including several on the Psalms.

RUFINUS OF AQUILEIA (ca. 345–411)

Born near Aquileia in northern Italy, Rufinus was sent to school in Rome where he became friends with Jerome. In later years, the two men would be separated by theological disagreements, but not before sharing a common commitment to the monastic life. From about 373, Rufinus spent seven years studying in Egypt and visiting the desert fathers. Together with Melania the Elder, a Roman noblewoman and widow, he traveled to Palestine, where the two founded a double monastery for men and women on the Mount of Olives. Rufinus became known especially for his copious translations of Greek theological writings into Latin.

THEODORET (ca. 393–ca. 460), Bishop of Cyrrhus

A native of Antioch, Theodoret was raised a Christian and educated in monastery schools. He became a monk himself before being elected Bishop of Cyrrhus in 423 (the ruins of the city now sit at the border between Syria and Turkey). While his diocese was only about forty square miles in size, he recorded that it was home to almost 800 churches. In addition to his service to those churches, which included building bridges and public buildings, the young bishop went on to become one of the most prolific writers of the Greek church. His works include histories of the church and the monks of Syria, and a series of commentaries on various books of the Bible, including the Psalms.

References for Quotations from the Church Fathers

Unless otherwise notated, all of the quotations from the church fathers are taken with permission from the following sources:

Psalms 1–50, edited by Craig Blaising and Carmen Harden. Copyright © 2008 by the Institute of Classical Christian Studies (ICCS), Thomas C. Oden, Craig A. Blaising, and Carmen S. Hardin. Used by permission of InterVarsity Press, P.O. Box 1400, Downers Grove, IL 60515, USA. www.ivpress.com

Psalms 51–150, edited by Quentin Wesselschmidt. Copyright © 2007 by the Institute of Classical Christian Studies (ICCS), Thomas C. Oden and Quentin Wesselschmidt. Used by permission of InterVarsity Press, P.O. Box 1400, Downers Grove, IL 60515, USA. www.ivpress.com

1   Taken from *Psalms 1–50*, 247.

2   Taken from *Psalms 51–150*, 63.

3   Taken from *Psalms 51–150*, 153.

4   Taken from *Psalms 51–150*, 254.

5   Taken from *Psalms 51–150*, 198.

6   Taken from *Psalms 51–150*, 343.

7   Taken from *Psalms 51–150*, 11.

8   Taken from *Psalms 51–150*, 61.

9   Taken from *Psalms 1–50*, 259.

10   Taken from *Psalms 51–150*, 428.

11 Taken from Psalms 51–150, 31.

12 Taken from Psalms 1–50, 314–315.

13 Taken from Psalms 51–150, 26.

14 Taken from Psalms 51–150, 45.

15 Taken from Psalms 51–150, 152.

16 Taken from Psalms 1–50, 50.

17 Taken from Psalms 1–50, 196.

18 Taken from Psalms 51–150, 219.

19 Taken from Psalms 1–50, 70.

20 Taken from Psalms 1–50, 236.

21 Taken from Psalms 1–50, 329–330.

22 Taken from Psalms 51–150, 162.

23 Taken from Psalms 51–150, 58.

24 Taken from Psalms 51–150, 281.

25 Taken from Psalms 51–150, 144.

26 Taken from Psalms 51–150, 178.

27 Taken from Psalms 51–150, 159.

28 Taken from Psalms 51–150, 55.

29 Taken from Psalms 51–150, 429–430.

30 Taken from Psalms 1–50, 229.

31 Taken from Psalms 51–150, 156–157.

32 Taken from Psalms 1–50, 178.

33 Taken from Psalms 1–50, 147.

34 Taken from Psalms 51–150, 167.

35 Taken from Psalms 51–150, 277.

36 Taken from Psalms 51–150, 420.

37 Taken from Psalms 51–150, 356.

38 Taken from Psalms 51–150, 172.

39 Taken from Psalms 51–150, 157.

40 Taken from Psalms 51–150, 202.

41 Taken from Psalms 51–150, 98.

NOTES

1 Dietrich Bonhoeffer, *Temptation* (London: SCM Press, Ltd., 1961), 33.

2 John Calvin, preface to *Commentary on the Book of Psalms, Vol. I*, trans. Rev. James Anderson (Edinburgh: Calvin Translation Society, 1845). Emphasis mine.

3 My friend read from the New International Version. Some scholars think the closing verse in that translation, as well as some others that are like it, is more accurate to the Hebrew than is the RSV or the NRSV.

4 C. S. Lewis, *Reflections on the Psalms* (New York: Harcourt, 1958), 63.

5 Martin Luther, "A Mighty Fortress Is Our God," trans. Frederick H. Hedge, 1853.

6 Verse 2 in the 1928 Book of Common Prayer version.

About Paraclete Press

Who We Are

Paraclete Press is a publisher of books, recordings, and DVDs on Christian spirituality. Our publishing represents a full expression of Christian belief and practice—from Catholic to Evangelical, from Protestant to Orthodox.

We are the publishing arm of the Community of Jesus, an ecumenical monastic community in the Benedictine tradition. As such, we are uniquely positioned in the marketplace without connection to a large corporation and with informal relationships to many branches and denominations of faith.

What We Are Doing

PARACLETE PRESS BOOKS | Paraclete publishes books that show the richness and depth of what it means to be Christian. Although Benedictine spirituality is at the heart of who we are and all that we do, we publish books that reflect the Christian experience across many cultures, time periods, and houses of worship. We publish books that nourish the vibrant life of the church and its people.

We have several different series, including the bestselling Paraclete Essentials and Paraclete Giants series of classic texts in contemporary English; Voices from the Monastery—men and women monastics writing about living a spiritual life today; our award-winning Paraclete Poetry series as well as the Mount Tabor Books on the arts; bestselling gift books for children on the occasions of baptism and first communion; and the Active Prayer Series that brings creativity and liveliness to any life of prayer.

MOUNT TABOR BOOKS | Paraclete's newest series, Mount Tabor Books, focuses on the arts and literature as well as liturgical worship and spirituality, and was created in conjunction with the Mount Tabor Ecumenical Centre for Art and Spirituality in Barga, Italy.

PARACLETE RECORDINGS | From Gregorian chant to contemporary American choral works, our recordings celebrate the best of sacred choral music composed through the centuries that create a space for heaven and earth to intersect. Paraclete Recordings is the record label representing the internationally acclaimed choir Gloriæ Dei Cantores, praised for their "rapt and fathomless spiritual intensity" by *American Record Guide;* the Gloriæ Dei Cantores Schola, specializing in the study and performance of Gregorian chant; and the other instrumental artists of the Arts Empowering Life Foundation.

Paraclete Press is also privileged to be the exclusive North American distributor of the recordings of the Monastic Choir of St. Peter's Abbey in Solesmes, France, long considered to be a leading authority on Gregorian chant.

PARACLETE VIDEO | Our DVDs offer spiritual help, healing, and biblical guidance for a broad range of life issues including grief and loss, marriage, forgiveness, facing death, bullying, addictions, Alzheimer's, and spiritual formation.

Learn more about us at our website:
www.paracletepress.com or phone us
toll-free at 1.800.451.5006

SCAN
TO
READ
MORE

Also available from Paraclete Press...

According to Your Mercy
Praying the Psalms from Ash Wednesday to Easter
Martin Shannon, CJ
978-1-61261-773-2 $14.99 Paperback

Many have called the psalms a "school of prayer." These ancient words from Scripture mirror our own thoughts and emotions—celebration and praise, suffering and lament, gratitude and asking for help—as relevant today as when they were first sung in the temple.

Fr. Martin Shannon brings deep teaching as well as the personal encounter of someone who has chanted and studied the Psalms for years. Each reflection is on one psalm, offering a meditation on its meaning and how it connects to our lives, followed by a word from one of the ancient church fathers and a prayer. There is a reflection for each of the forty-seven days from Ash Wednesday to Easter that reflect the various twists and turns on the Lenten journey.

Readers will discover the power of the Psalms to inspire their own Lenten journey toward Easter.

Your Light Gives Us Hope
24 Practices for Advent
Anselm Grün, OSB
978-1-61261-904-0 $16.99 Paperback

A daily reader of simple and direct Advent reflections. Anselm Grün shows the reader how to approach the festive season consciously, making it a blessed time for ourselves and our families.

He draws on his experience as a spiritual director to offer practices for personal devotion or for family prayer for each day of Advent. Also included are special reflections for the Sundays of the season.

Anselm Grün's titles have sold more than 15 million copies in 30 languages. This title brings his spiritual wisdom to North American readers who are eager for a new voice among titles for the Advent and Christmas season.

Available through your local bookseller or through Paraclete Press:
www.paracletepress.com; 1-800-451-5006